Raised Bed & Container Gardening Handbook For Beginners

Successfully Growing Your Own Self-Sufficiency Garden with Healthy Vegetables and Fruits, Using Companion Planting and Gardening Tips

Collin Bradford

Copyright by Collin Bradford 2022 - All rights reserved.

The content contained within this book may not be reproduced, duplicated, or transmitted without direct written permission from the author or the publisher.

Under no circumstances will any blame or legal responsibility be held against the publisher, or author, for any damages, reparation, or monetary loss due to the information contained within this book Either directly or indirectly, you are responsible for your own choices, actions, and results.

Legal Notice:

This book is copyright protected. This book is only for personal use. You cannot amend, distribute, sell, use, quote, or paraphrase any part, or the content within this book, without the consent of the author or publisher.

Disclaimer Notice:

Please note the information contained within this document is for educational and entertainment purposes only. All effort has been executed to present accurate, up to date, complete, and reliable information. No warranties of any kind are declared or implied. Readers acknowledge that the author is not engaging in the rendering of legal, financial, medical, or professional advice. The content within this book has been derived from various sources. Please consult a licensed professional before attempting any techniques outlined in this book.

By reading this document, the reader agrees that under no circumstances is the author responsible for any losses, direct or indirect, which are incurred as a result of the use of the information contained within this document, including, but not limited to, errors, omissions, or inaccuracies.

Leave a review about our book:

As an independent author with a small marketing budget, reviews are my livelihood on this platform. If you enjoyed this book, I'd really appreciate it, if you left your honest feedback. You can do so by clicking review button.
I love hearing from my readers and I personally read every single review!

Table Of Contents

Introduction 7

Part 1 - Getting Started 9

Chapter 1: Planning Your Garden 11
    Build a Simple Raised Garden Bed: Everything You Need to Know 11
    Reasons to Have a Raised Bed Garden 12
    Factors to Consider Before Building a Raised Bed Garden 15
    Where to Plant 18
    Site preparation 19
        Container Gardening 21
        Where to Keep Container Plants? 22
        Right Container for Gardening 23
        Soil for Container Gardening 25

Chapter 2: How to Build a Raised Bed Garden 27
    Select a Size 27
    Frame the Raised Bed 28
    Line the Bed 30
    Fill with Soil 30
    Types of Raised Bed Gardens 31
    Concrete Raised Bed 31
    Square Foot Bed 32
    Hot Raised Bed 33

Chapter 3: Basic Soil Science for Successful Vegetable Gardening 35

Chapter 4: Soil Composition and Maintenance 41

Chapter 5: Watering and Irrigation 49
    Water Regularly 49
    Water According to the Weather 49
    Consider your Plants' Watering Requirements 50
    Water Deeply, not Frequently... 50
    Water in the Morning 50
    The Ideal Way to Water 51
    Irrigation System for Raised Bed Gardens... 51
        How does Drip Line Irrigation Work?... 52

Weeding 101... 53

Chapter 6: What is Companion Planting? 57
    The Science Behind Companion Planting 57
    Benefits of Companion Planting.. 58
    Companion Planting Strategies 60
        Companion Planting with Herbs 61
        Flowers as Plant Companions.. 63
    Companion Planting Chart... 65
    Beginner's Mistakes to Avoid 68

Part 2: Growing Fruits, Berries, and Vegetables 71

Chapter 7: The Best Vegetables for a Raised Bed 73

Chapter 8: Top Fruits and Berries for Raised Bed Gardening 102

Chapter 9: Tips & Tricks for the Best Garden 114

Chapter 10: Common Mistakes 120

Planting Calendar 125
- Yearly Summary 125
- Planting and Seeding 127
- Companion Plants 129
- Planting and Seeding 129
- Weekly Watering Planner 131
- Plant Growth Progress 135
- Garden Task and Planning 136
- Harvesting Log 138
- List of Gardening Tools 140

Conclusion 145

Introduction

Limited space will no longer come between you and your passion for gardening. With raised bed gardening, you can grow plants in smaller spaces. There are plenty of locations which can be converted into a full-fledge garden by investing a little time and money. Raised bed and container gardens not only provide an alternative to traditional gardens, but they give your place a very modern and contemporary look. You can create such a garden with a pattern and design that could easily match the theme of your outdoor living space. Through this Handbook, I will explain to you exactly how you can make it happen.

Part 1 - Getting Started

Chapter 1:

Planning Your Garden

Are you thinking about planning your own raised bed garden? This initial stage is the most crucial one because this is the time when you select your garden site, consider all the important factors, including the budget, list all the materials to buy, deci de the design and layout of your garden, the type of plants you want to plant and ways to manage all the logistics to pull out this task successfully. In this chapter, let me walk you through the process, starting from the basics!

Build a Simple Raised Garden Bed: Everything You Need to Know

When we say "raised bed garden " or simply "raised bed," we're talking about a freestanding box or frame that rests above-ground in a sunny position and is filled with good-quality soil. Anyone can build a raised bed using the most easily accessible material. There can be one single raised bed or multiple beds in your garden, depending on the space available. Usually, the bottom of raised bed is left open so that the plant roots can access soil nutrients below the ground level. Of course, a raised bed doesn't have to be complicated: you can make one without a structure by simply mounding the soil 6 to 8 inches high and flattening the top.

What are Raised Bed Gardens?

A raised bed garden is built on top of your existing ground or garden soil. Then the structure is filled with additional soil. A raised bed can be built at different heights. Typically, there is enough space around the edge of each bed to be able to walk around it, rather than step in it, allowing the soil to remain loose and fluffy, rather than compacted. This is vital because roots grow best when air and water can flow freely through the soil.

Typically, raised beds have frames, but you can choose what kind of frame you want. Raised bed frames are typically built of wood or durable plastic, but they can also be made of stones, cinderblocks, bricks, patio pavers, broken concrete pieces, corrugated metal, straw bales, and so on. To put it another way, you can make one match your own style and surroundings, using either new or old materials. You don't even have to do any building from scratch if you'd rather not because raised beds are also available in kits. You can install the beds as per the given guidelines.

Reasons to Have a Raised Bed Garden

It's not just the space-saving that makes the raised bed garden the right option. There are many other benefits of planting in raised beds. Here are some convincing reasons:

Less weeds

Such a garden is raised above the ground level. This allows you to employ weed barriers in the garden box, which can be placed between the ground and the soil. It is easy to work on weeds in each individual bed and remove them on a regular basis.

Improved Soil all the Time

When you plant a garden in the ground, you're limited to using the soil that's already there. It's possible that the soil isn't ideal for gardening. You can improve the soil by adding mulch and compost, but this is a difficult task to do. Whereas in the case of the raised bed garden, you can fill it with the soil that is appropriate for your particular plants. The existing soil can even be changed and replaced in the raised bed every few months to ensure better growth.

Easier to Control Pests

Pest control is relatively easy when it comes to raised bed gardening. You can simply place chicken wire beneath the raised garden and above the box to keep out animals like squirrels, ground hogs, and moles. This will successfully keep these pests away from your valuable plants. Other pests like plant bugs can be kept by planting pest repellant plants in each raised bed.

Better Portability

You can move a raised garden box anywhere in your yard. This is useful if you want to improve the look of your yard by landscaping. You can move the frame to a different location and then fill it with the soil.

Good Accessibility

In a traditional garden, some plants are difficult to access because of their placement in the yard. Sometimes it is difficult to trim or prune the damaged parts of the plants because they are hard to reach. But the best part about raised beds is that you can access every plant in the yard with ease. This makes it simple to water, weed, examine, and harvest the plants.

Increased Yields

When you can add good soil, remove the weeds easily, and water the plants properly, then nothing can stop you from getting higher yields. You can have that when you plant in raise beds. You can manage all the factors responsible for the better growth of the plants.

Cost-Effective

Seeds can be very costly. When planting in a typical "in-ground" garden, it's common to start by dispersing seeds. Only a few seeds then grow into a plant, whereas others get wasted. But in a raised bed garden, you sow limited seeds at particular places, which all usually grow into a plant.

Extended Growing Season

The temperature of the soil determines your planting season. In the spring, the soil in a raised garden box will warm up considerably faster than ground soil which can mean to can plant a little earlier than the start of the planting season.

Appealing to the Eye

Your raised garden beds will look neat and tidy at all times. You can set the garden beds to make a fine patio and create a walking path with grass, stones or pebbles in between the beds.

Factors to Consider Before Building a Raised Bed Garden

There are a lot of factors that you need to consider before setting up a garden, especially if it's a raised bed. While deciding on the design and the layout of the garden, here is what you should need to know first:

Size of the Raised Beds

The average size of a raised bed is 3-4 feet by 6-8 feet. This allows you to reach into the raised bed from the side to plant, dig, and weed without having to step into the garden and perhaps compact the soil. Height is also an important consideration. If you're going to install your raised bed on a hard surface, such as a driveway or over compacted soil, make sure it's deep enough for plants to root (particularly root veggies like beets and carrots). If the depth is too shallow, then the plant roots will reach through the subsoil (or hard surface) and hit a brick wall. I normally advise at least 12 inches.

Lumber (such as cedar) usually comes in a standard size of 6 inches in height. To put it another way, the dimensions of a standard board are 2 feet by 6 inches by 8 feet. The two boards could also be stacked. Two stacked 2 x 6 boards have a height of 12 inches.

You can absolutely make it taller (18 inches, 24 inches, or 36 inches), but keep in mind that the extra soil will put a strain on the sides. Any raised bed that is more than 12 inches tall will require cross-supports.

Consider what you want to grow. The depth of the soil is critical, as it determines how much soil depth the crop requires below ground. Carrots, potatoes, parsnips, tomatoes, and squash, for example, require a soil depth of 12 to 18 inches. If plants don't have loose soil to this depth, their roots won't be able to reach the nutrients they need. A minimum soil depth of 6 inches is required for shallow-rooted crops such as lettuce, assorted leafy greens, and various types of onions.

It would be good to just ensure that your beds have a depth of 12 to 18 inches. This would be a to secure choice. Whatever frame height you choose, you'll need to soften the dirt below the ground to accommodate it. If you want to grow a tuber or a root vegetable in a bed that is 6 inches high, loosen the soil below the earth roughly 6 to 9 inches more. There's no need to do this if you're merely planting shallow-rooted plants.

Location

The location of a raised bed garden is crucial, but it doesn't have to be in your backyard. Your raised bed could be placed in a sunny side yard, front yard, balcony, or driveway. If you have a slope, you'll want to make adjustments and see how the area drains.

Grass Removal

How do you remove the grass to clear the ground? That is one good question, as it is a common problem. If you've ever attempted to remove grass from the ground, you understand how difficult it is. An easy technique to get rid of grass is to draw a line around the area and cover it with a layer of cardboard, then cover it with dirt. The grass will eventually decompose, and voila! A new garden location. If you do this in the fall, everything will break down throughout the winter.

Irrigation System

You might want to do this before your raised bed areas are built and filled if you want to set up a complete drip irrigation system with a line running from your faucet or rain barrel. This allows you to run hoses beneath walkways or layers of mulch and adapt the bed to the location of the hose's connection to the irrigation system.

Soil

There are a few online soil calculators that will help you figure out how much soil you'll need to fill your raised bed. When it comes to soil, I recommend getting the best quality you can afford when planning a raised bed garden. A triple soil mix with organic veggie compost on top is a nice combination.

Framing

Installing a couple of halfway pegs to keep the beds from shifting over time is something that needs to be done initially. This is one of my most important raised bed suggestions!

Where to Plant

For best yield, most plants require at least eight hours of full sun per day. The more sunlight you have, the better, so plant your garden in the sunniest part of your yard. Avoid low-lying, rainy areas, as the soil gets too damp. During the growing season, you'll need convenient access to a hose because your garden will need to be watered.

The most important component of a thriving garden is healthy soil. Because you may fill your raised bed with a soil blend that is superior to the native soil in your yard, raised beds to give you an immediate advantage over a traditional garden. Your plants' roots will be able to develop freely in loose soil that is rich in minerals and organic matter, ensuring that they have access to the water and nutrients they require for healthy growth. Raised beds must be placed in areas that receive plenty of sunlight. An ideal place meets the following requirements:

- 6 to 8 hours of direct sunshine each day, particularly after lunch
- The terrain is level and even
- Close to the house for weeding and harvesting convenience
- Do not place your bed in a frost pocket or in a windy region
- Avoid any wet or swampy places since soil needs to drain efficiently

Site preparation

To create a basic raised bed, draw a line with string around the area where you want it. Keep it between 3 and 4 feet wide, so that you can easily reach the center. It helps if the grass in the area has been smothered, but if there is still sod or grass in place, mow it fairly short and dig it out, saving the clumps. Loosen the dirt in the bed, turn the clumps of sod in the bed upside down, scrape soil off the pathway around the sides and put it on the bed.

Site Preparation without Digging

Some gardeners do not bother to dig the turf out. As long as the soil is thick enough, it will keep the grass and weeds beneath it out. Charles Dowding was the gardener who invented the "no-dig" approach. Digging, according to him, brings more weed seeds to the surface of the earth, resulting in more weeding. His claim is that digging also hastens nutrient loss, necessitating more frequent feedings, and it breaks away the intricate life and fabric of your soil, limiting its ability to drain and hold moisture.

Grass or weeds should be mowed as near to the ground as possible. Cover the area with cardboard, which will suffocate the grass and weeds and gradually decompose into the soil. To prevent weeds from slipping through cracks, overlap the cardboard/newspaper by about 6 inches. They'll grab whatever sunlight they can get their hands on. Cover that cardboard with a thick layer of compost about 4 to 6 inches high. This will be the medium in which you will be growing your plants.

Now you can start planting right away. By the time roots reach the cardboard, they will have begun to decompose, allowing the roots to seek deeper than the cardboard layer.

Through the activity of worms and other organisms, the compost you place on top should eventually get integrated with the soil beneath. Each fall/winter, top up the raised beds with fresh organic matter about an inch or two thick, which will assist in progressively increasing the fertility and health of the soil.

Building Raised Beds on Compacted or Contaminated Soil

Digging below the ground is often necessary for soils that have been affected by compaction or have other issues, but it only needs to be done once. This is especially crucial for deep-rooted crops like carrots, which thrive in soil that has been loosened and modified down to 10 to 12 inches in order to allow air and water to reach the roots. Remove the top layer (approximately a shovel's depth or 10 inches) after mowing the grass fairly short and digging it out; it may be easier to work in rows.

All rocks, old roots, and plant detritus should be removed. To loosen up the earth, dig a little deeper with the shovel (a few more inches). Organic materials, such as compost should be added to the soil. Compost should make up roughly 25% of your soil. Then replace the top layer and combine the dirt layers on top. Your ground and soil are ready for planting.

Container Gardening

Those of us who don't have space for raised beds or a large garden plot can still grow our own food using container gardening. Want more control over your growing environment and fewer weeds? Container gardening is an effective method to make the most of your gardening space while also simplifying your duties. A container garden has the advantage of being able to be placed practically anywhere. Gardening in containers, even if it's just one or two pots on the side of your driveway or in the corner of your balcony, allows you to make the most of your available space. Consider elements like sunshine exposure, water accessibility, and wind protection when determining where to put your containers, just like you would with a regular garden bed.

Where to Keep Container Plants?

To get the most out of your veggie yield, make sure your pots are in full sun (i.e., 6 to 8 hours of sunlight per day). Lettuce, spinach, and other leafy greens can thrive in less sunlight (3 to 5 hours each day), but full sun is ideal for fruiting plants like tomatoes, peppers, squash, and eggplant. The most sunlight and warmth will come from southern and western exposures, while northern and eastern exposures will be shadier and cooler.

It's also a good idea to place your pots in an area where you can water them with a hose. Remember that container gardens require more water than traditional in-ground gardens, and there's nothing like lugging a watering can across your yard a dozen times every morning—and then doing it again in the evening! It will definitely save a lot of your time and work if you have an easily available source of water nearby.

Containers that are shielded from direct wind are less likely to dry out and are less likely to tip over. As the season progresses, depending on the size of your containers and the plants you're cultivating, they may become top-heavy, making them more vulnerable to toppling over in severe winds. Place containers in protected areas or prepare to secure them (e.g., with cinderblocks, stones, or ropes).

Finally, consider the various microclimates on your land. Microclimates are little pockets of space where the immediate climate differs from the overall environment of your place.

An asphalt driveway, for example, would retain warmth longer than a patch of grass, so any pots placed on the tarmac will benefit from the extra warmth. On the one hand, this may cause the pots to dry out more rapidly, but on the other hand, the warmer soil may help the plants develop better.

Right Container for Gardening

The most important aspect of container gardening is—surprise, surprise—choosing the appropriate container! Almost anything that retains soil can be gardened in, from plastic pots and cinderblocks to whiskey barrels and wheelbarrows. When it comes to cultivating a healthy container veggie garden, however, there are three crucial considerations to make when selecting a container:

Good Drainage

A plant container must have a drainage hole or another method of allowing water to pass through it. Bacterial and fungal development thrive in wet soil, stifling plant productivity or killing them outright. Gardeners in drier climates may want to use containers that hold more moisture, while those in more humid climates may want to choose containers that allow for more air flow.

Suitable Size

In general, the more root area you can provide, the better your plants will thrive. Huge pots are suitable for growing large veggies, like beefsteak tomatoes or squash. Keep in mind, however, that larger containers are heavier and more difficult to handle and may be too heavy for a balcony. Little containers are portable, but they also dry out more quickly, necessitating greater attention on hot days.

Material

The container's construction is the final significant item to consider. Containers now exist in a variety of shapes and sizes, each with its own set of benefits and drawbacks. The following are some of the most common container materials:

Plastic: Plastic pots are available in a wide range of shapes, colors, and sizes, making them one of the most popular container gardening options. Plastic pots are also the most cost-effective option. They're quite light, keep moisture well, and are simple to clean and reuse for multiple gardening seasons.

Pots made of ceramic (terra cotta) are another common option. They're not only more beautiful than plastic pots, they're also a lot heavier—especially when full of soil. The fundamental difference between glazed and unglazed ceramic pots is that glazed pots hold more moisture than unglazed pots. The wonderful thing about ceramic pots is that the clay is porous, allowing some air and water to pass through. This keeps the soil from being too wet, but it also means that soil in (unglazed) clay pots dry up faster than soil in plastic containers.

Fabric: Fabric pots have grown in popularity in recent years as a result of their low weight and breathability. They frequently come with handles as well, making transporting them around a breeze. They may also be washed and reused with relative ease. The fabric allows air and water to move freely through it, which benefits plant roots by encouraging them to become more fibrous and hence more efficient at absorbing water and nutrients. Fabric pots have a disadvantage in that they dry out rapidly, necessitating frequent watering.

Again, virtually anything may be utilized as a container, so think outside the box. Herbs, strawberries, and cherry tomatoes grown at eye level can be readily maintained and gathered in hanging baskets, which make effective use of excess space.

Use whiskey barrels, buckets, baskets, boxes, bath- and other tubs, window boxes, and troughs—**anything that can hold soil.** Just make sure that the planting container has drainage holes at the bottom and is the right size for you.

Soil for Container Gardening

Healthy soil is required to grow healthy plants. In order to foster healthy root growth and provide a decent harvest, container plants require the finest possible nutrients, aeration, and drainage.

Garden soil should not be used! Most garden soils are overly heavy, easily waterlogged and compacted, and disease and insect breeding grounds. Instead, use a "soilless" potting mix designed exclusively for container use. It will be quick-draining and light, and it will be free of illnesses and pests.

To give nutrients, soilless potting mixes typically contain a combination of peat (or coconut coir), perlite, and vermiculite, as well as other ingredients such as crushed limestone and granulated fertilizers.

Chapter 2:

How to Build a Raised Bed Garden

Now that you have cleared the ground and it's ready to build the raised bed, you can start gathering the materials to set up each bed. Remember that they are filled with soil that gets damp, and the roots penetrate inside as the plant grows, so they must be surrounded by suitable structures. Building a raised bed garden involves a few bases.

Select a Size

Examine your yard and pick what you want to grow, then set up a bed where it will receive adequate light; edibles, for example, require at least six hours of sunlight. The length of the box will be determined by the amount of space available, but the width is critical: you want to be able to weed and reach plants without crushing them or compacting the soil. If it's against a wall or fence, keep it under two and a half feet wide, or five feet wide if you can reach in from both sides. Each bed should be at least a foot deep.

Frame the Raised Bed

Corten steel, stones, or bricks can all be used to build a raised bed, but wood planks are the most frequent and easiest to work with for novices. Choose rot-resistant cedar, cypress, or black locust lumber that hasn't been treated. Avoid pressure-treated wood, which has been maintained with chemicals that can leech into your soil—especially if you plan to produce food.

You can edge your raised beds with any materials you have on hand, including wood, stones, bricks, and cement blocks. Avoid using painted or pressure-treated wood because it might leach chemicals or lead into the soil. End-to-end bricks can be used along the edges, or if you have enough, put them on end to create taller bed sides.

- **Cinderblocks**

Cinderblocks work really well for Mediterranean herbs like rosemary and lavender. The extra heat generated from concrete is ideal. The holes in the blocks can be filled with soil mix, and herbs or strawberries can be planted in them. Each block is 16 inches by 8 inches, and the cost is very inexpensive at big stores.

- **Pallets**

As long as you know where they originated from, pallets are a cheap source of garden bed materials. Pallets are used to transport materials. Avoid pallets that have been treated with methyl bromide, an endocrine-disrupting substance that can have an effect on your reproductive health. Although most pallet manufacturers stopped using the chemical in 2005, numerous obsolete pallets remain on the market. On the pallet, look for a stamp that says "HT" or "heat-treated." Do not use the pallet in your garden if there is no stamp or if you cannot verify an HT on the surface.

- **Railroad Ties**

Railroad ties are easy to use because they are simply laid out on the ground and held down with iron spikes. Most of the creosote leaches away. Old railroad ties treated with creosote do not appear to pose any health risks.

- **Stones and Rocks**

Some regions have plenty of rocks and stones, which create excellent free edging. You can start building the bed around the soil mound you've already built. You can then fill up the sides with extra dirt and add compost, shredded leaves, manure, and other materials. Smooth the top and set it aside until next spring, when it will be ready to plant.

- **Wood Composites**

Wood composites are a relatively new product made of recycled plastic and wood fibers. It's rot-proof and long-lasting, but it's also quite expensive.

- **Untreated Wood**

Pine is the most affordable untreated wood. Like many untreated kinds of wood, it can rot after a few years. Hemlock, on the other hand, has a longer shelf life. Resistant-to-rot woods, such as cedar, redwood, and locust, can last much longer, but they are more expensive. The best choice is cedar, which is rot-resistant and long-lasting, lasting 10 to 15 years. Because of the oils in the wood, it is also insect-resistant. Although recycled wood created from plastic bottles is costly, it will last a long time. Another option is to buy untreated wood boards that are significantly thicker. A 2-inch-thick board of larch wood, for example, can survive a decade without treatment. Chemicals are used in modern treated wood to keep it from decaying.

Line the Bed

Leave your ground soil visible if it is healthy. If you reside in a city where lead or other pollutants are a problem, or if you wish to plant on a patio or other concrete surface, spread weed-blocking fabric over the bottom of the bed before you set it. This water-permeable cloth keeps the nasty stuff out while keeping your soil in place. You can also opt for a raised bed with legs that are elevated off the ground.

Fill with Soil

Fill your box with a mixture of topsoil and compost, leaving approximately an inch of space below the top of the frame. A six-foot-by-four-foot-by-13-inch-deep bed, for example, will require around one cubic yard of dirt. Remember to top off your beds with extra soil and compost every year. Your raised bed is ready to plant!

Note: There are many garden beds available that you can order and assemble if you don't want to build them from scratch.

Types of Raised Bed Gardens

The construction of the raised bed garden may differ depending on the type of beds you want to build. Here are some options that you can consider:

Concrete Raised Bed

A concrete block raised bed is inexpensive and simple to construct, and it's a fantastic method to add raised vegetable beds to your yard quickly. The best feature is that your raised bed may be built just on top of the lawn!

Concrete blocks are a low-cost option for raised beds. The blocks are only approximately $1 each at a local store. So, for under $20, you could build a great sized raised bed for planting. Of course, this does not include the cost of soil, which will almost certainly be the most expensive component of this process.

Although constructing a raised bed with concrete blocks is simple, there are a few steps to ensure that your Do-It-Yourself raised garden beds look their best and fit where you want them to. You must first choose a location for your concrete raised bed garden. Choose a location that is relatively flat and receives lots of sunlight. Then decide how many concrete blocks raised beds you have room for, keeping in mind that you'll need plenty of space between them so you can easily access and stroll between them.

Designing a concrete block raised bed couldn't be easier because we're utilizing square blocks that are of the same size. All you have to do now is measure the size of the area you want to put it in. You can build numerous beds of the same size if you have a large space. Consider how easy it will be to work in your concrete block raised garden beds as you develop your design. You don't want the raised beds to be too wide because getting to the middle can be challenging. Also, allow a few feet between each bed so that you have enough area to walk and move around. This is especially critical if, like us, you want to put your raised gardening beds right on top of the grass and need to mow in between them.

Square Foot Bed

Square-foot gardening is a type of raised bed gardening that consists of a square-shaped raised box. Instead of planting in typical rows, square-foot gardening involves planting in 4x4-foot blocks. Different crops are planted in different blocks based on their sizes, such as 16 radishes per square foot or one cabbage per square foot. To clearly differentiate each square foot, a lattice is put across the top.

SFG beds are typically at least 4 feet by 4 feet in size, with a square foot lattice on top to visibly dividing the crops. The beds can be as small as 2x2 feet or as large as 4x12 feet, but the most frequent size is 4x4 feet. This enables plants to be placed closer together.

There are no plant spacings to memorize in order to keep the planting process easy. Instead, depending on the size of the plant, each square contains 1, 4, 9, or 16 plants, which are easily placed in each square by drawing a tiny grid in the dirt with your fingertips.

SFG is a great fit for a lot of scenarios. The joys of fruit trees, growing vast crops of potatoes in barrels, or managing a greenhouse full of high-value crops can all be experienced with this type of raised bed.

Hot Raised Bed

A hotbed is a raised bed that is layered with decomposing straw, manure, or other organic matter. To develop plants or seeds, you place a thinner layer of growing medium (soil/compost) on top. A hotbed, like any other compost heap, is made up of organic elements. There should be a nice mix of nitrogen-rich 'green' and carbon-rich 'brown' components in the ideal soil. A hotbed can be placed indoors or outside in a covered garden construction such as a greenhouse, polytunnel, or even a garden building or conservatory. The location of your hotbed will eventually be determined by where you live and the growing conditions in your area. Obviously, it will also be determined by the mechanics of your site and the amount of space available.

If you live in a particularly cold climate, keeping your hotbed under cover is a wonderful option because it doubles your protection. It's critical to avoid placing your hotbed in a highly windy area or in a frost pocket. If you live somewhere with a warmer winter, this level of protection and care can be excessive. When it comes to choosing a site for your hotspot, you have more options.

It's a good idea to put your hotbed somewhere close to your house. You won't want to walk too far in the winter to check on, harvest, and care for your winter crops. It is also best to keep your hotbed close to materials sources. The proximity of a water supply is another factor to consider. Watering your winter plants will be easier and more convenient if you are close to a water supply.

Materials for a Hotbed

The sides of a new hotbed are best made of reclaimed bricks. After you've chosen a place for your hotbed, you'll need to consider the methods and materials you'll need to build it. Let's start with a look at the various alternatives for your hotbed's edges. The material you employ to keep the materials inside will obviously affect the hotbed's heat retention capabilities. You might want to think about using:

- Stone
- Bricks
- Concrete
- Clay
- Plastic containers

The new hotbed's boundaries are built up around a base of wood chips. The method for creating the boundaries of your hotbed will, of course, be determined by the materials you use. However, gathering those resources will be the initial step. Knowing how much/how many materials you'll need will be beneficial. You'll need to decide on the size and shape of your hotbed, as well as how deep it will be. The contents of your hotbeds should be at least 31.5 – 47.5 inches deep for best results. This will provide enough materials to provide the required heat, as well as a top layer in which to grow plants or sow seeds.

Chapter 3:
Basic Soil Science for Successful Vegetable Gardening

Soil is a medium that is a mix of bacteria, microorganisms, nutrients, and minerals which aid plant growth. Each plant requires the right mix of all those elements. For successful gardening, we need to understand what good soil really means. Let's dissect some of the factors that make a quality soil:

Nutrients

There are three macronutrients that are critical for plant growth: Nitrogen (N) stimulates foliage growth, phosphorus (P) aids in the formation of robust root systems and blooming, potassium (K) aids in disease resistance. Zinc (Zn), Boron (B), iron (Fe), manganese (Mn), copper (Cu), molybdenum, and chlorine (Cl) are some of the other micronutrients that help plants thrive.

Proper pH

Plants thrive in soils with a pH balance of 6.5 to 7.5, or even as high as 8.4 if the soil has iron, zinc, copper, and manganese micronutrient levels. But there are exceptions. Blueberry plants are acid-loving, and they grow at a lower pH, while some legumes need a higher than average pH.

Moisture Content and Drainage

Plants thrive on well-draining soil in general. This means that the soil is not packed and compacted, allowing water to flow freely. The simplest way to determine how efficiently your soil drains is to dig a hole that is 12 to 18 inches broad and equally deep. Fill the hole halfway with water and drain it. Fill it up once it's been totally drained. Soil that drains well drops around 1 inch each hour.

Type of Soil

The type of soil in the container also has an impact on your plant-growing abilities. Soils are classified into four categories:

1. **Sandy soil** drains well but holds rainfall and minerals poorly.
2. **Clay** is a thick material that stores nutrients and water effectively, but it drains poorly. Roots and microbes struggle to thrive as a result.
3. **Silt** is a blend of sand and clay that can bind together like soil.
4. **Loam** soil is a mix of sandy soil, clay and silt, and it is good for most vegetable and flower gardens. Its textured surface allows it to drain

properly while preserving moisture and nutrients. It also supports a wide range of microorganisms, including bacteria and fungi.

Some plants, particularly native American plants, have evolved in a variety of soil types and may require more clay-like or sandy soils to survive. The texture of the soil is given a lot of thought. While overall soil texture is significant, a closer look at maintaining a healthy soil mixture is more critical. Over-tilling can result in the loss of concentration, which is the way soil particles link together.

How to Tell if the Soil is Healthy?

Test your soil to see what you have and what you don't. It can be done by a professional or an inexpensive at-home soil test which evaluates nutrient and pH levels. Either way, you'll have an excellent notion of what you're up against and what you'll need to do to adjust your soil. Observing your plants can also reveal a lot. If there isactivity in the garden, you will know if your soil is okay. Earthworms in the soil, pollinators nibbling away, and/or root systems branching out, are the easiest evidence that your plants are growing.

Soil Sampling and Testing

A soil test is one of the finest techniques to ensure that the garden will be a success. Only a soil test can accurately identify how much lime and fertilizer should be applied to the garden. However, the sample must be collected appropriately if the soil test information is to be valid. Collect samples with a tiny trowel or shovel.

Collect samples from eight to ten different spots throughout the garden. The soil should be dry or, at the very least, devoid of moisture. Vertical slices of the 4 to 6 inches of top soil should be collected. Fill a clean plastic bucket halfway with soil and thoroughly mix it. Metal containers, as well as those tainted with detergents or other foreign matter, can result in incorrect recommendations.

When taking a soil sample, stay away from any uneven spots in the garden. Collect soil samples away from standing water, sites where large volumes of ashes have been dumped, or regions where debris has accumulated. Collect samples from the garden's most representative regions for the most reliable results.

Every year, soil samples should be taken. Keep in mind that the observed patterns might be more meaningful than the absolute results. You won't be able to observe trends if you sample in the fall one year and the spring the next. You are not fertilizing enough if the soil test results show a persistent drop in phosphate and potassium levels. You are over-fertilizing if the findings reveal high increases in phosphate and potassium levels. The goal of effective soil fertilization is to gradually raise the soil's nutrient levels and then keep them at a medium or high test result.

How to Fix Soil

Chemical insecticides, which can affect your garden's food web, as well as pollinators and birds, should be avoided. Chemical fertilizers should be avoided because they can disrupt the natural feeding connection between plants and soil microbes.

Liming to Fix the pH

Lime should be applied to the garden based on the results of a soil test. The pH of the soil should be adjusted to the proper range with proper liming (6.0 to 6.5 for most vegetables). The right soil pH encourages root development, optimises nutrient availability, and prevents the occurrence of certain physiological abnormalities (blossom end rot) and illnesses (Fusarium wilt). Over-applying lime limits nutrient availability and produces nutritional imbalances, so don't go overboard.

Apply ground limestone per 1,000 square feet of garden space is recommended by a soil test report. If hydrated lime is utilised, it should be used at a rate of three-quarters that of ground limestone. Hydrated lime reacts with the soil more quickly. It is, however, more expensive and difficult to disseminate. The best time to use ground limestone is a few weeks before you plan to sow your garden. Lime can be sprayed prior to the establishment of the cover crop if soil samples are taken in the fall. A fall treatment allows the lime to react with the soil for several months before planting. However, if lime is indicated, it is preferable to apply it right before planting rather than not at all. Spread lime evenly over the garden, working it into the top 6 inches of soil. A lime treatment should not be needed more than every two to five years, depending on the soil type, fertiliser usage, and environmental circumstances. To suppress insects, do not apply high amounts of lime around the base of plants or sprinkle it over them. This approach has the potential to raise the pH above the optimum level, resulting in lower production.

Pre-plant Fertilization

Apply fertilizer to garden spaces as directed by the soil test results. Use two to three pounds of a fertilizer or its equivalent per 100 square feet of garden area in the absence of a soil test. Distribute the fertilizer equally across the soil surface and work it into the top 6 inches.

Soil Preparation

Garden soils will not work if they are excessively wet. It is too damp to work if water can be squeezed out of a handful of soil or if the squeezed lump of dirt does not split apart when dropped. When working with damp soil, clods form that become exceedingly hard as they dry, making them unsuitable for seedbeds. Clods restrict soil-to-seed contact, which can drastically impair the germination of vegetable crops, particularly small-seeded varieties. Working some soils early enough in the spring to plant cool-season crops by the optimum planting date may be problematic. Drainage ditches, tiling, sand addition, and organic material integration have all been used to improve these soils.

Fall Soil Preparation and Ridging

Another option is to work a section of the garden in the fall and create 6- to 8-inch high ridges. The ridges will warm up and dry out faster than the rest of the garden due to the increased surface area and improved drainage. However, keep in mind that these ridges will remain dryer throughout the growing season, so irrigation may be required later on. These ridges can typically be used for the earliest planting without any additional tillage or preparation, if fertilizer is supplied in the fall. When employing this system, nitrogen will be lost.

Chapter 4:

Soil Composition and Maintenance

Soil qualities such as texture, drainage, and organic matter content can be modified by varying the contents of the raised bed. It is suggested that you use a soil and compost mix with a 70:30 ratio of soil to compost. Make sure the soil and compost you're using are of good quality and come from reliable suppliers. Although the initial set-up has the greatest impact on overall soil health, there are various techniques to improve and maintain soil health over the life of the raised bed.

Keep Soil Covered

The protection of the soil habitat is the focus of this idea. If the soil is left exposed, it is considerably more vulnerable to erosion and temperature variations, both of which can stress plants and soil creatures. To assist and extend the growing season, covering crops (an unharvested crop produced as part of a rotation plan to give conservation advantages) can be utilized. Covering crops can make a difference, even on a small scale, by increasing organic matter, preventing erosion, conserving soil moisture, providing nitrogen for future crops, suppressing weeds, and even reducing compaction. Mulch, which comes in a variety of forms, such as black plastic, plant wastes, and compost, is another approach to keep the soil covered. Mulch lowers evaporation and increases the quantity of rain or irrigation water that penetrates the soil.

Maximize Plant Diversity

Every grower should rotate their crops at least once a year. More diversified plants support a wider range of soil animals and microbes. This aids in the disruption of disease cycles as well as the stimulation of plant growth. Covering crops can also help achieve this goal. If residues are left on the surface of the soil, organisms digest them, releasing nutrients back into the soil. This increases nutritional availability as well as organic materials.

Maximize the Period of Living Root Growth

This principle has everything to do with keeping the soil covered. The soil should ideally be covered with living plants that have living roots. Raised beds are designed to grow crops for longer periods of time because they are not insulated by the surrounding soil. This allows for earlier planting and a longer growing season. Planting winter-hardy crops, employing row covers or cold frames, and mulching are other strategies to extend the growing season. The soil organisms are fed by the cycle of ongoing growth and the die back of plant roots. Living roots also help to prevent soil erosion and keep moisture in the soil.

Add Compost

Compost is an organic matter that has been decomposed, and it is the most effective way to increase the health of your garden soil. Working compost into the soil feeds the soil, improves soil structure, allows nutrients to be retained, promotes good drainage while also absorbing water deep in the soil, keeps soil loose so air can reach the roots of plants, helps preserve a neutral pH, and defends plants from many common garden diseases. Earthworms or other microbial life in the soil are also fed by compost. The worms will tunnel into the soil to improve aeration and drainage while also increasing soil fertility by leaving behind their castings. Here are other things that you can use as compost:

1. **Leaves:** One of my favorite ingredients is well-aged, shredded leaves. They're free (which I appreciate as a frugal person) and add a lot of bulk. So, what exactly do I mean when I say "well-aged"? It means old rotten leaves that are ready to be decomposed. If you don't have enough leaves on hand, ask around.
2. **Mineralized soil blend** is readily accessible and, in most cases, regionally sourced. Therefore, the composition may vary depending on your location. Granite is abundant in the Atlanta area; hence granite dust is used in the majority of mineralized soil blends.
3. **Vermicompost** (Worm Castings): When I introduced worm castings to my garden, it made a huge difference. Buy it if you can get it in a bag in any quantity. It's worth it, even if it's not widely available or inexpensive. Thankfully, a small amount goes a long way. It won't take much to make a significant effect.

Worm castings are far higher in all of the essential nutrients that your plants need to thrive. They provide five times the nitrogen, seven times the phosphorus, and ten times the potassium than the regular topsoil.

Castings offer another level of complexity to the overall soil composition. To put it another way, this media is one of my best-kept secrets for making very productive garden soil.

Vermicompost (composted worm dung) will provide another layer of organic richness to your raised bed gardens. For years, it's been one of my not-so-secret soil success weapons.

4. **Mushroom Compost** is an organic material that is dark brown in color and flexible. It is not formed of mushrooms. It's a byproduct of the substances used to cultivate the mushrooms — what's left over after they've been harvested. Mushrooms are produced in natural materials such as hay, gypsum, maize cobs, cottonseed hulls, and so on. However, it gets light-weighted and porous by the time it's composted, packed, and marketed as mushroom compost. It includes about 3% nitrogen and potassium, as well as a small amount of phosphorus and other beneficial nutrients such as magnesium and calcium. This compost won't affect the pH of your soil because it's a neutral pH (6.5-7.0).

5. **Ground Bark**: There are many different types of ground bark to pick from, but pine is the most prevalent. Despite the fact that pine bark is a little acidic, I've never seen it having much of an impact on the overall pH of my garden soil. For your raised bed gardening, make sure you utilize old bark. During the earliest phases of decomposition, freshly chipped wood will deplete rather than benefitting your soil.

Ground bark is a good source of carbon. It will degrade over time, and its gritty texture allows water and oxygen to flow freely through your garden beds. Ground bark has a wide range of particle sizes, which can help your plants thrive.

Composted Cow or Poultry Dung: Because of the nutrients, organic matter, and diversity of particle matter that it provides to complement overall soil make-up, well-composted animal manure has been a mainstay of organic soil fertility for thousands of years. That isn't going to change. What has changed are farming practices and the potential of manure contamination as a result. Even well-composted manure can include synthetic herbicides that are still active when put into today's garden soil. As a result, I advocate using cow or poultry manure, rather than horse manure.

> Buy composted cow or poultry manure by the bag from a reputable supplier. Buyer beware, whether it's an off-brand or you're buying in bulk. Many people, including myself, have poisoned their soil with killer compost by accidentally adding herbicide-tainted compounds commonly found in horse dung.

Get a Soil Test

Composting isn't something you do once and then forget about. It is all part of the soil's ongoing nutrient renewal process. Every few years, conduct a soil test to see what additional nutrients are required to boost plant development and productivity. Soil test kits are online and at garden supply stores and are simple to use. You can also take samples of soil to your local county extension office for a more detailed analysis.

Levels of potassium (K), Soil pH, calcium (Ca), phosphorus (P), magnesium (Mg), and Sulphur (S) are all measured in a basic soil test. A soil test will also reveal the amount of organic matter and lead in your soil, as well as advice for altering these levels.

You can enrich your soil with organic additions for a boost of nutrients once you understand the nutrient deficits in your soil. Alfalfa meal, for example, can enrich the soil with nitrogen, phosphorus, and potassium. Worm castings are an excellent nitrogen source. Phosphorus and calcium are found in bone meals. It requires a regular dose of all-purpose organic fertilizer.

Add Mulch

Mulch is essential for vigorous plants and healthy garden soil. It promotes natural plant growth by retaining soil moisture, keeping the soil cold, and preventing weed growth. The mulch will decay over time, adding organic matter to the soil and increasing its richness.

Prevent Soil Compaction

Hard, compacted soil will not enable water and nutrients to penetrate, leaving the soil barren and dry. Plants dehydrate and starve because their tiny roots can't extend out in search of moisture and nutrition. Microbiological activity, which is required to convert organic matter to nutrients that feed plants, is also hampered by compact soil.

Garden beds should be 3-4 feet wide so you can reach all regions without treading on the dirt. Allow enough space between the beds for a wheelbarrow or a manual lawnmower to pass through if you want to keep the grass in your walks, about 2-feet minimum.

Crop Rotation

Planting crops in new garden places each year reduces nutrient depletion, and disrupts pest and disease cycles, keeping the garden soil healthy. Potato pathogens are an excellent illustration of how crop rotation helps to maintain the health of garden soil. During just one growing season, nematodes and fungus that produce scabby skin areas on potatoes multiply rapidly in the soil. This year's crop may not be impacted, but if next year's crop is put in the same spot, the ravenous disease organisms from the previous season will devour it. If disease spores and organisms do not feed on their favored crop, they will naturally die out.

For all garden crops, use the three-year rule. Each year, rotate crops such that the same vegetable family is not produced in the same location for three years. That allows soil pathogens enough time to die. Some plants also help to improve the health of the soil. Nitrogen is added to the soil by peas and nasturtiums. After growing nitrogen-consuming crops, you can restore the soil by planting nitrogen-producing crops.

Grow Cover Crops

Although cover crops are generally produced to improve the soil, some of them can also provide food. Plant a cover crop at the end of the gardening season and allowing it to stay in the garden over the winter provides the garden with a number of benefits. The soil is protected by a cover crop from eroding due to heavy rain, winds, and snow melt-off. During the mild winter months, the crops will also minimize soil compaction and weed growth.

Kale, turnips, radishes, and other broad-leaf greens are excellent cover crops and food suppliers during the winter months. Clover, ryegrass, lentils, and peas are other excellent winter cover crops. In the spring, turn any residual crops under to act as green manure. After being turned under, the cover crop plants will decay, increasing soil fertility.

Add Aged Animal Manure

To boost the health and fertility of your garden soil, add seasoned animal dung. Fresh animal dung is too hot for plants, and it may include germs that are dangerous to humans. Allow several months to a year for the manure to mature before adding it to the garden soil. When put into garden soil, chicken, cow, rabbit, horse, goat, sheep, and bat droppings are high in nutrients and improve soil structure.

Chapter 5:

Watering and Irrigation

All plants thrive on water, though their water needs might vary. Over-watering or under-watering are the two worst things that can stifle a plant's growth. Proper watering needs a proper irrigation system, and that's what this chapter is all about! First, let me share a few general tips on watering the plants, and then I will discuss some tips on how to set up a working irrigation system for a raised bed garden.

Water Regularly

It is important to watch the watering system while it's running, no matter what method you employ for watering. Set your irrigation system to operate when you're in the garden if you have one. If you are in your garden when it is being watered, you can spot problems such as a dead battery or a defective timer, a leak in a line, over-watering, or under-watering before the health of your plants is damaged or water is lost due to flood, etc.

Water According to the Weather

Plants require extra water when it is dry, windy, and hot outside. In hotter climates, such as Arizona, raised-bed gardening may require daily watering. During other seasons of the year, the raised beds may only need to be watered once or twice a week. When altering the frequency of the timing, seasonal conditions should be considered.

Consider your Plants' Watering Requirements

For healthy crops, adequate moisture is required. A plant has 75 percent to 90 percent water to live healthily, which is utilized for photosynthesis, structural support, and the movement of nutrients and sugars to different sections of the plant. To decide how often to water, look for indicators of under-watering stress, such as brown dry-leaf edges, poor growth, leaf curl, wilted or fallen leaves, or branch dieback. Heat stress and not watering stress, causes plants to wilt in the afternoon, but recover in the morning. By not over-watering your plants, you can help them acquire some heat resistance. Soft decaying roots, persistently damp soil, pale green or yellow new growth, leaf curl, and leaf drop are all signs of overwatering. Problems arise as a result of inconsistent watering.

Water Deeply, not Frequently

Water deeply enough to wet the plant's entire root system. Shallow irrigation that does not cover the entire root system discourages healthy root growth. Plants should not be watered excessively. After watering, assess the watering depth using a soil probe (any long metal item, such as a long screwdriver). If the probe glides easily through the dirt, it's damp. If not, the soil is likely to be dry, necessitating more regular watering. Allow the top 1-2 inches of soil to dry out before watering again. Every now and again, it's a good idea to water twice as long to flush the salts out of the root zone and soil.

Water in the Morning

In the morning, plants absorb moisture more efficiently. Early morning watering hydrates plants before the heat of the day. Watering in the morning also prevents waterborne infections and pests, which can happen if you water at night.

The Ideal Way to Water

Water raised-bed gardens in a steady and even manner. The best technique to irrigate raised beds is to use an automatic watering system. During the warmer months of the year, timers can be set to water every day or less frequently, depending on rain and other weather conditions. Watering seldom causes seeds and seedlings to dry up and perish, as well as water-stressing grown plants, which attracts pests and diseases. Watering is a costly aspect of gardening. Finding the best approach to water raised beds can aid in water conservation rather than waste.

Irrigation System for Raised Bed Gardens

Soaker hoses, sprinklers, and drip lines connected to a timer are examples of automatic watering systems. In my garden, I've tried all three ways and found that drip-line irrigation is the most efficient way to irrigate raised-bed gardens.

- Soaker hoses are prone to become blocked, cracked, and not always watering evenly.
- By getting the leaves wet, sprinklers in the garden can encourage and spread illness. Excess evaporation occurs when water is sprayed, and it may not always reach the soil and evenly hydrate the root zone.

Drip lines irrigate the earth rather than the plant. Drip lines also deliver water at a consistent rate, allowing the soil to absorb it with little waste or evaporation.

How does Drip Line Irrigation Work?

Drip line irrigation systems, often called trickle irrigation, are one of the most popular ways of irritating plants. It is simple to set up and use, and it aids in the reduction of disease problems connected with varying amounts of moisture on plants. It has also proven to be effective since the water can seep into the soil before evaporating. Second, instead of being sprayed everywhere, the water drips directly to the roots of the plants, where it is needed, thanks to a network of pipelines, tubes, and emitters.

Grid Drip Line Irrigation

The Grid Irrigation System is a pre-configured irrigation system that is intended to set up in minutes and can be used in both ground and raised garden beds. The Garden grid drip irrigation. Pictured above, is one good example. You can buy a complete kit with the tubes, pipes, joints, hoses and timer in one pack as per the size of your raised beds. The drip lines are installed in a grid-like pattern, and a water inlet is attached to the grid. The water flow is regulated through a timer. This grid can be easily removed and installed back in when the soil is replaced in a raised bed.

The technique was developed after a couple attempted to install drip lines in a square foot garden and discovered that not only did it appear unkempt, but it also wasn't nearly as successful as they had hoped. The Garden Grid was created to make drip irrigation for home gardeners easier and more comfortable, as all that is required to set it up is to spread it out and connect it to a garden hose, with no need to cut tubing, add connectors, or insert emitters (or the use of soaker hoses). The drip system not only functions as a watering system, but also works as a planting grid for laying out garden beds.

Garden Grids come in a variety of grid sizes ranging from 2'x2' to 4'x6', and they can not only be expanded as your garden grows but several grids can also be joined with the addition of a valve and connecting hoses.

Weeding 101

Weeds are one big challenge that every farmer and gardener have to face. Weeds can grow in raised bed gardens as well, and here are some pointers that you should keep in mind while dealing with the weeds.

Weed after Rain

If I had one piece of advice to give a gardener, that would be to weed after it rains. When the soil is damp rather than dry, it is much easier to uproot plants—and get all of the roots out. I understand that drought is a problem in many regions, but if you do get rain and there are a lot of weeds, get out there before the soil dries out again. The entire process will be a lot simpler, quicker, and more thorough.

Know What Weeds You're Dealing With

Before you take any action, be sure to know what kind of weeds you're dealing with. You need to know if a weed is toxic to touch, if it's an invasive species, if it's an endangered species, or if it's an important habitat for another animal, bird, or bug. You can search the plant's cultivar through image searching on Google. Upload its image and learn about it before removing it from your garden.

Recognize How the Weeds Spread

You can stop a weed from propagating if you know how it reproduces. Roots or rhizomes, on-ground runners, or seeds are used to propagate most plants. If a weed reproduces by seed, it must be removed before the blooms fade and seeds develop. You must cut off a weed's paths if it spreads by runners.

Some common weeds generate massive rhizomes or tap roots. Digging up deep-rooted weeds may appear to be a sensible option, but it might backfire. The loosening of the soil can sometimes foster the growth of any roots that have been left in the earth.

Protect Your Skin as Well as Your Clothing

There's a lot to consider out there! Ticks, mosquitoes, poison ivy, and oak are just a few examples. Also, be aware of the possibility of allergic reactions. Wear gloves, long sleeves and long pants, a garden apron to cover your clothes. Wash them (including your shoes) in separate loads as soon as you're done weeding or clearing brush. Even if you don't come into contact with poison ivy, the oil can flow through your clothing.

Also, before scratching your nose, remove your gloves! I've been there, forgotten to do that, and next I had a rash to prove it! The correct equipment makes the process a lot easier, and maybe even better. Which tools are most effective will be determined totally by the weeds you're dealing with.

If pulling the weeds doesn't work, smothering may be necessary. This sounds ominous, and it's certainly not a quick fix, but if weeds are invasive and the problem is large, you may need to smother the entire growing area. The entire garden bed, as well as a few feet around it, is covered in thick layers of UV-stabilized plastic, weighted down with large weights, stones, or rocks, shutting off everything a plant needs to survive—water, air, and light. The covered plants might take months or even years to die off, depending on how tenacious the plant is. The trick is to be patient and never give up!

It Isn't Finished Until All of the Weeds Have Died

So, you've removed the weeds from the garden. So, what's next? And all of those weeds are still conspiring and strategizing to return to haunt you. Your disposal options will be limited by what is allowed in your area. The idea is to keep the plants isolated until they are completely dead and unable to regenerate. You may put them in a rubbish pile, bag them and 'cook' them in the hot sun for a few months, burn them, or bring them to a yard waste disposal facility. Again, it depends on what is considered safe, ethical, and legal in your area.

Chapter 6:

What is Companion Planting?

The concept of growing diverse plants together for mutual benefit is known as companion planting. Although most studies on the benefits of companion planting have focused on vegetable gardens, ornamentals, such as roses, can also benefit from it to help reduce disease and pest infestation. Companion planting, unlike other aspects of gardening, is often based on observations. It's a case of trial and error to figure out what works best for you. Understanding your garden as a biodiversity system in which all plants are interrelated and dependent on one another, on the other hand, might help you make smarter plant choices.

The Science Behind Companion Planting

Plants use semiochemicals (pheromones or similar chemicals) to send signals to other plants and to insects. For instance, a plant under attack by insects may release what's known as herbivore-induced plant volatiles, or HIPVs, into the air to indicate to other plants that it is time to put their chemical defenses up. HIPVs can also lure in beneficial insects that prey on those pests, such as attracting ladybugs to come and eat aphids.

Semiochemicals may also contribute to "canopy shyness," which is how some plants refrain from touching other plants in close proximity. Plants can also communicate via mycorrhiza, the fungal organisms that colonize almost every root on the plane.

Using the mycorrhizal network underground, a tree can send signals to other trees that can influence things like the kind of pollinators that show up.

Benefits of Companion Planting

Companion planting has various advantages. Beneficial insects and pollinators are attracted to plants, which also discourage pests and act as insect repellants. They have the ability to defend themselves against predators and unwanted creatures. Cucumbers, for example, are unappealing to raccoons.

Companion planting also help to improve soil fertility by increasing nutrient delivery, availability, and uptake. Tall plants, such as corn, can give shade for crops that don't fare well in the hot summer heat, such as lettuce, and they can also provide support for trellising crops. Interplanting diverse crops can help you distinguish between fast-germinating plants, like radishes, and slower-germinating plants, like lettuce, in your garden. Companion planting can even assist in keeping weeds at bay. There are several other benefits, such as:

Reduced Pest Pressure

The most sought-after benefit of companion planting is the reduction of pest damage. Countless studies have been conducted on everything from how pests discover their host plants to tactics for diverting pests away from desired crops before they can cause major harm. To keep vegetable garden damage to a minimum, companion planting to lessen pest pressure employs attracting, capturing, fooling, and discouraging pests.

Weed Pressure is Reduced

Another possible benefit of some companion planting schemes is a reduction in weeds without the use of herbicides. Allelopathy is a science that can be utilized to control weed development in the garden. Through crowding and shadowing, companion plants can also act as a living mulch, reducing weed pressure.

Reduced Disease Pressure

Companion planting is being researched for its capacity to control certain plant diseases, which is surprising. Though the interplay between disease organisms and the plants they impact does not appear to be as well-explored as other aspects of companion planting, it can be influenced by particular companion planting tactics.

Improved Soil Fertility or Structure

Green manures and cover crops have been employed as companion crops with vegetable and grain crops for a long time, but mostly in bigger agricultural operations. When implemented appropriately, even on a small scale, home gardeners can profit from these soil-building tactics. Certain plant partnerships, such as those geared at breaking up heavy clay soils or enhancing the condition of the soil through the presence of root exudates, can help improve soil structure (compounds produced and excreted by the roots of living plants). Other companion planting practices aid in nitrogen transfer, which helps to improve soil fertility.

Improved Pollination

By boosting the number and diversity of pollinators in the region, companion plants can improve garden harvests. Pollination rates could be enhanced by carefully selecting plant relationships that attract and nurture the specific kinds of bees known to pollinate target crops.

Improved Biological Control

An increase in the quantity and diversity of the numerous beneficial insect species that eat common garden pests or utilize them to house and feed their developing babies is another advantage of certain companion planting approaches. Plants that attract and sustain pest-eating insects work well together in the garden, resulting in better biological control and fewer pest outbreaks. Companion plants can give necessary sustenance in the form of pollen and nectar, as well as provide a habitat for these "good" bugs. Plant partners can also be chosen for their ability to operate as "banker" plants, which are produced specifically to attract and support pests so that beneficial insects can feed on them when pest populations in crop plants are low. By giving beneficial insects a reason to stick around, this strategy may help improve or equalize the seasonal population of beneficial insects.

While monocultures have their place in the garden on occasion (think slope-covering ground coverings), you'd be hard-pressed to find a gardener or garden visitor who doesn't prefer a mixed planting to a monoculture. Home gardens, unlike farms, where row planting is required to facilitate mechanical harvesting, are ideal locations for a mixed-planting design. The aesthetics of companion planting come with extra benefits since tiered gardens with several layers of plant structures and many growth behaviors, from ground coverings to trees and everything in between, are more welcoming to a larger range of insects and other creatures.

Companion Planting Strategies

Make sure that you are following crop rotation regulations before you start thinking about companion planting in your garden. Planting the same garden crop in the same location for multiple gardening years might result in pest and disease problems, as well as nutrient imbalances.

The knowledge of which plants make suitable companion plants for each other varies widely, depending on the source you examine. There are only a few "hard truths" that everyone agrees on, such as the advantages of planting maize, pole beans, and pumpkins all at the same time. The corn supports the beans, which extract nitrogen from the air for the crop's roots. In the dappled shadow of the corn, the pumpkins discourage weeds and keep the ground cooler, conserving water.

Companion Planting with Herbs

Not every garden has enough space for cultivating a diverse range of crops for companion planting. But that doesn't mean you can't make use of herbs' many advantages, such as catching and repelling pests, and attracting pollinators and other beneficial insects, to boost biodiversity in your garden.

These are just a handful of the culinary herbs that help control pests or attract beneficial insects in your garden, ranging from aphids to tomato hornworms:

- Basil
- Borage
- Chives
- Cilantro
- Lavender
- Mint
- Oregano
- Rosemary
- Sage
- Thyme

Also, allow some of the herbs to bloom, as this is when they attract beneficial insects in droves.

Common Examples

Tomatoes and basil are not only great friends in cooking, but also in the garden. Basil has been demonstrated to resist certain insect pests, such as thrips, and to confuse the moths that spawn tomato hornworms. Researchers also discovered that interplanting tomatoes with basil reduced armyworm egg-laying. Basil also attracts bees, which helps pollinate tomatoes and increases their health and flavor. Ladybugs, which consume minor garden pests like aphids and spider mites, are attracted to dill.

Borage attracts pollinating bees and goes well with tomatoes. Borage complements strawberries wonderfully, adding to their sweetness and vibrancy.

Aphids, ants, and flea beetles are all deterred by mint. Simply put mint in its own pot or bed nearby, as it is a highly aggressive grower!

Nasturtiums keep hungry caterpillars away from brassicas, like cabbage, broccoli, and kale, so plant them near those plants. Nasturtiums also keep blackflies away from fava beans.

Parsley attracts beneficial insects to preserve and pollinate tomatoes. Plant these herbs in the same row as the tomatoes.

Hoverflies are attracted to poached egg plants (a wildflower), which suppress aphids on surrounding lettuce.

Sage is a helpful plant for warding off carrot flies. It's also a good idea to grow it around a cabbage patch to keep cabbage moths away.

Flowers as Plant Companions

Planting flowers in your vegetable garden accomplishes more than just providing aesthetic value and cut flowers. Nasturtiums, sunflowers, marigolds, and zinnias are annuals that repel pests and attract beneficial insects, while lavender is a perennial.

Common Examples

- Cucumbers and pole beans go well with sunflowers. Sunflowers give support for climbing plants, as well as shade for crops that can become sun-stressed in hotter climes.
- Pest-eating beetles, like ladybugs and ladybirds, as well as predatory wasps, are attracted to tansy. But tansy also repels a variety of pests, including cutworm, which damage asparagus, beans, cabbages, carrots,

celery, maize, lettuce, peas, peppers, potatoes, and tomato plants. Tansy is a perennial; therefore, it only needs to be planted once, and will come back year after year. What more could you ask for in flowers for your garden?

- Increase the number of blooms! Aphid-eating hoverflies will be attracted to tiny parasitizing wasps if calendula or cosmos are grown nearby. Marigolds are also great for attracting pest-eating beneficial bugs
- Garlic and garlic spray have a strong odor that repels a variety of insects. Garlic is poisonous to aphids, which harm over 400 plants. Onion flies, ermine moths, and Japanese beetles are all deterred by garlic. Plant pieces of garlic cloves between rows of potatoes, besides fruit trees, and alongside lettuces and cabbages.

Companion Planting Chart

	Vegetable	Perfect Combinations	Not To Pair With
1	Asparagus	carrots, basil, dill, coriander, marigolds, tomatoes, parsley	onions, garlic, potatoes
2	Basil	beans, asparagus, bell peppers, beets, chili peppers, cabbage, marigolds, eggplant, potatoes, tomatoes, oregano	rue
3	Beans	carrots, beets, cabbage, chard, cucumbers, corn, radishes, peas	onions, garlic
4	Beets	broccoli, bush beans, Brussels sprouts, cauliflower, chard, cabbage, onions, kohlrabi	field mustard, charlock, pole beans
5	Broccoli	beets, basil, carrots, bush beans, chamomile, celery, dill, cucumber, lettuce, garlic, mint, marigolds, onions, nasturtiums, rosemary, radishes, spinach, Swiss chard, sage, thyme	cantaloupe, asparagus, mustard, peppers, climbing beans, strawberries, pumpkins, watermelon, sweet corn
6	Cabbage	celery, beets, lettuce, chard, onions, spinach	tomatoes, kohlrabi

7	**Carrots**	beans, lettuce, onions, peas, peppers, tomatoes	dill
8	**Corn**	cucumber, climbing beans, peas, marjoram, squash, sunflowers, pumpkins, zucchini	tomatoes
9	**Cucumbers**	beans, borage, lettuce, dill, nasturtiums, oregano, radish, sunflowers, tansy	Potato, melons, basil
10	**Lettuce**	basil, cabbage, beets, chives, carrots, onions, poached eggplants, radishes, scallions, spinach, strawberries	broccoli, cabbage, cauliflower, kale, brussels sprouts, or kohlrabi
11	**Onions**	carrots, cabbage, lettuce, chard, tomatoes, peppers	peas, beans
12	**Peas**	corn, cucumber, mint, radish, turnip	onions, shallots, garlic and potatoes
13	**Peppers**	basil, carrots, marjoram, oregano, tomatoes	beans, peas, cauliflower, kohlrabi, broccoli, cabbage, kale, brussels sprouts
14	**Potatoes**	beans, basil, corn, celery, horseradish, garlic, marigolds, lettuce, peas, onions, spinach, radishes	asparagus, broccoli, cauliflower, cabbage, cucumbers, Brussels sprouts, eggplant,

			carrots, peppers, kohlrabi, squash, melons, strawberries, raspberries, tomatoes, sunflowers
15	**Pumpkin**	beans, marigolds, corn, squash, nasturtium	potatoes
16	**Radishes**	cabbage, beets, chives, carrots, kale, cucumbers, spinach, lettuce, squash	hyssops
17	**Squash**	corn, beans, marigolds, dill, peas, nasturtiums, strawberries, radishes, sunflowers	potatoes
18	**Spinach**	beans, brassicas, cilantro, eggplant, peas, strawberries	potatoes
19	**Strawberries**	caraway, bush beans, lettuce, chives, spinach, sage, squash	peppers, eggplants, cabbage family, potatoes, tomatoes
20	**Tomatoes**	carrots, asparagus, onions, celery, peppers, parsley	dill, corn, potatoes, kohlrabi
21	**Zucchini**	corn, beans, garlic, dill, nasturtiums, marigolds, peas, oregano, spinach, radishes	potatoes and pumpkin

Beginner's Mistakes to Avoid

Companion planting works differently for each set of plants. There are tons of factors involved in making a plant pair grow successfully together in a place. One little mistake can ruin your whole companion gardening experience. Here are some of the mistakes that you should avoid:

- Plants that compete for fertilizer needs, water, space (above-ground growth and below-ground root systems), and sunlight should not be planted adjacent to each other in general.
- Drought-tolerant plants, like rosemary and snap peas, should not be placed near water-loving plants like sweet corn and lettuce. Cabbage will stifle tomato growth since the two plants compete for nutrients in the soil. When planted together, bell peppers and fennel will likewise fail to thrive for the same reasons.
- Crops vulnerable to the same plant disease, such as blight, should be maintained as far apart as possible to prevent the disease from spreading. Pests are the same way.
- Some plants can stifle the growth of others. Fennel is frequently cited as an example of a poor companion plant that should be kept separate from all other crops in the garden.
- Planting the wrong ones can have a severe impact on your crops' health. Planting tall plants, such as bush beans or pole beans and tomatoes together, for example, is a bad idea since they will compete for light, with the tomatoes having a better chance of winning.
- Finally, some plants are thought to be allelopathic, which implies they interfere chemically with rival plants' chemical important systems. Garlic and onions, for example, are supposed to inhibit the growth of beans and peas. Sunflowers are said to inhibit the growth of potatoes and beans.

- When cabbage and cauliflower are planted together, they usually don't do well. However, there is little empirical proof that plants engage in "combatant" behavior,

Putting plants in the soil together at random, even if they are recommended as companions, is rarely a smart idea and may even lower your crop production. Tomatoes, for example, may crowd out the basil planted beside them, resulting in a smaller basil crop than if the basil had been planted alone. So, consult the professional gardeners and learn more about the most popular planting companions before growing them.

Part 2: Growing Fruits, Berries, and Vegetables

Chapter 7: The Best Vegetables for a Raised Bed

Harvesting the freshly grown vegetables of your very own garden gives every gardener joy. There is nothing more satisfying than growing your own food in your yard. Guess what? You can grow plenty of vegetables in your raised bed garden as well. Such a garden is suitable for planting small plants, vines, shrubs, herbs, and bushes. Here is the list of the vegetables that are easy to grow.

Cabbage

If you don't have a lot of space for a garden, a 4 × 4 square foot or raised bed garden is great for growing cabbage.

A 4-foot-wide raised vegetable bed allows for easy maintenance from both sides. Depending on the amount of room available, the length might range from 4 to 20 feet or longer. When the heads of your growing cabbage are firm, harvest them.

Sow cabbage seeds 1/2 inch deep and 1 inch (2.5 cm) apart; thin to 18 to 24 inches (45-61 cm) between rows. Transplant the cabbage plants to the garden when they are 4 to 6 weeks old and have 4 to 5 genuine leaves. Plants with lanky or twisted stems should be buried 1 to 2 inches (2.5-5cm) below the top two pairs of leaves.

In rows 24 to 36 inches (61-91cm) apart, space seedlings 18 to 24 inches (45-61cm) apart. Plants can be placed closer together because the cabbage heads get smaller with maturity. Plant cabbage in the early spring, with black plastic or garden fabric in place to warm the soil. To layout transplants, cut an 'x' in the fabric. Plant the successive crops every two weeks.

In an in-ground garden, the spacing between rows should be 24-36 inches. Plants should be spaced about one foot apart in a 12-inch soil depth.

Sow the seeds closer than the desired final spacing when planting directly in the garden. Thin the seedlings to 12 inches apart as they mature. Buying "transplants," or miniature cabbage plants that are already growing, can help you save space and effort in the yard. In late April, you may pick up these baby cabbage plants at your local garden center. If necessary, you can keep a transplant in a container until there is space in the garden.

Cabbage Seeds

If beginning from seeds, plant cabbage seeds about 4-6 weeks before transplanting them. Transfer to the garden with a ball of dirt around the roots; bare-root transplants are more likely to produce seed heads. As the root system of this plant is shallow, handle it gently. Mulch to keep moisture and weeds at bay. To sustain development, feed lightly every few weeks. Cabbage can withstand light frosts and freezes. This plant can withstand temperatures as low as 32 degrees, while 60-65 degrees is the ideal growing temperature. Because of its strong absorption of nitrogen and potassium from the garden soil, it's ideal to rotating your cabbage crop every season. This provides time for the soil to restore its nutrients.

Carrots

Carrots are the second-best vegetable to plant in a raised bed because they thrive in loose, moist soil. A raised bed's loosely packed soil provides the ideal growing environment for carrot tubers. The type of raised garden bed you should prepare depends on the type of carrots you wish to grow. Carrots that grow taller will require a deeper bed. Smaller and shorter carrots, such as the French carrot variety, will just require a low and short bed.

You should sow carrot seeds 3 to 5 weeks before the last spring frost date if you desire a summer crop. Remember to plant a new crop of seeds every three weeks in the late spring season if you want a continual yield. Sow seeds in the mid-to late-summer season if you want a fall harvest. The optimal time to begin is around 10 weeks before the first frost of the fall season.

It is not good to disturb the roots of a fully grown carrot plant. It is advisable to disperse the seeds at the time of sowing and let them grow directly in the raised bed rather than transplanting them. Carrot seeds should be placed one-fourth inch deep and two to three inches apart in the soil. The proper spacing is required to ensure that your carrot plants receive enough nutrients to produce a higher yield. Carrot spacing is important since it can prevent excessive thinning.

To keep the soil moist for the carrot seed, frequent shallow watering is required. You can examine the moisture level of the soil with your finger. To prevent a crust from forming on the top of the soil, spread a layer of fine compost on the raised bed. Have patience; it takes two to three weeks for carrot seeds to germinate.

Beetroot

It's no secret that homegrown beetroot tastes considerably better than store-bought beets. The optimum time to plant your first batch of beets is in the early spring. Because you're growing in a raised bed, you can get a head start on planting. If you're growing beets in the ground, you'll need to wait until the soil is ready to use.

Draw a line in the raised bed's soil about ½ inch deep and plant one seed every 2 inches apart. Water after covering the seeds with soil and gently firming them down with your hand.

Beetroot can be easily transplanted. It isn't one of those plants that dislike being disturbed.

Alternatively, put beetroot seeds a half-inch deep in the raised bed. The space between the seeds in the rows should be 1 to 2 inches. After sowing, cover the seeds with a layer of soil and space the rows one foot apart.

Keep in mind that each wrinkled beet seed is actually a cluster of two to four seeds. When the young plants reach a height of 4 inches, they must be thinned.

Plants should not be pulled during thinning. The roots of the plants may be disrupted in this manner. So, simply cut the greens off.

Keep your soil wet for quick seed germination. Soak the seeds before planting if you want them to germinate quickly.

Tips for Caring for Beets

Because each seed produces many seedlings, thinning is required. Thin the seedlings 3 to 4 inches when the tips of the beetroots are 4 to 5 inches tall. Pulling the leaves from the ground may disturb the roots, so pinch or cut them off.

Apply a layer of mulch to the soil to aid in the retention of moisture. Water the roots once a week, about 1 inch. Beetroots require moisture, so use your finger to test the soil's dryness.

Grass clippings can also be used to sprinkle around your beet plants. These clippings include a small quantity of nitrogen, which is beneficial to beetroots. It will also assist in the retention of moisture and the protection of plants from weeds.

Beets require a sufficient amount of nutrients, particularly phosphorus. You can use fertilizer to meet the needs of beet plants and observe the effects in the form of improved plant growth.

Use a shade cloth to keep beetroots from bolting in the heat. When you encounter weeds, be patient with young plants because weeding can easily disrupt the weak roots of beets.

Lettuce

As a plant that does not thrive in a weedy environment, lettuce thrives on raised beds.

It is considerably easier to keep weeds under control in a raised bed. Weed control in a traditional garden bed can be tough. Warm soil is another feature of a raised bed that this vegetable enjoys. Because raised beds are warmer, you can sow your lettuce seeds a little sooner. This is also conceivable because lettuces do not mind being exposed to colder temperatures for a short length of time.

You'll be able to keep your seeds going and grow for a little longer and later into the season if you sow them early. The germination process will also be aided by warm soil. There is a type of lettuce for everyone, with so many varieties to choose from! In the early spring, sow lettuce seeds directly into your raised bed. Also, make sure the soil is evenly hydrated. After that, you should be able to harvest your lettuce in just thirty days. This is true for the majority of lettuce cultivars. Harvest your lettuce in the morning for maximum benefit.

The flavor of the lettuce is said to be preserved by doing so. You'll get more out of your lettuce plant if you only harvest the leaves, you need rather than eliminating the entire head.

Kale

The best time to plant is determined by the climate in which you live.

The seed packet has all of the necessary information and directions for growing kale seeds. If you want a summer crop, the optimum time to plant kale is in the early spring. Plant it in the garden 3-5 weeks before the latest frost date. If the temperature is really low, the young seedlings should be covered. Young plants are unable to withstand the cold on cool evenings. Plant the kale 6-8 weeks before the first fall frost if you want a fall crop. You don't need to worry about the frost because it enhances the flavor of the leaves.

Seeds or seedlings can be used to grow kale. You can either spread seeds directly in the raised bed or plant seedlings. Sow the seeds 14 to 12 inches deep in the soil. Leave 8 to 12 inches between the seeds. The soil should be light and well-drained. Seedlings that are young and slender will appear in two weeks. If you're transplanting seedlings, make sure they're planted at the same depth as they were in the pot. The kale seedlings should be spaced 18 to 24 inches apart.

Radishes

Summer radish seeds can be planted from early March to the end of May. If they are shielded from excessive heat, they can be seeded until September.

This is commonly accomplished by spreading seeds near taller plants that will shield them from direct sunlight. In July and August, winter radish seeds are planted. Oriental/Chinese radish is often planted in late August to September, though new types are more heat resistant.

The same method is used for sowing all varieties of radish. Create a shallow hole in the raised bed soil and sprinkle the seeds in. Add a little dirt on top and press it in. In one to two weeks, the seedlings will emerge.

Summer radishes can be seeded in raised beds and containers, with 5 cm/2 in between plants and perhaps 7 cm/3 in between rows. Oriental and Chinese radish, on the other hand, require more space; leave 30 cm/12 in between two plants. As these plants may take greater space, I would recommend planting only 1-2 plants per raised bed.

Bok Choy

Another vegetable that doesn't like to share space with weeds is Bok Choy. These plants require a lot of food, but grow quickly. They flourish in light, loose soil that is rich in nutrients. Bok Choy is a simple-to-grow vegetable that appreciates cooler climates. This veggie should be grown in a pot in indirect sunlight. You can then put the seedlings onto your raised bed once the frost has passed. Bok Choy needs to be shielded from the cold, even if it is their favorite environment. This implies that they should be planted beneath a plant that will provide some shade and protection.

When Should You Plant?

Bok Choy is a fast-growing vegetable that is normally started from seeds and planted directly into the garden after the threat of frost has passed, or four weeks before the last frost. After the risk of frost has passed, you can also purchase nursery seedlings to put in the garden.

It takes some practice to figure out when to sow Bok Choy so that it doesn't go to seed in its first season. If the weather is excessively hot, this vegetable will bolt (send up flower stalks), but it can also bolt if exposed to temperatures below 50 degrees when it is young. In locations where springtime is cool but soon warm, it may be beneficial to start seeds indoors and then transplant seedlings outdoors once the threat of frost has passed. If you plant Bok Choy in the late summer or early fall, when temperatures are somewhat consistent, you may have a higher chance of preventing bolting.

Choosing a Planting Location

The planting location must have well-draining, healthy soil that can be saturated by rain. Especially if it's a fall crop, the site should get full sun for the majority of the day. A spring crop, which is more difficult to grow because of the plant's proclivity to bolt in response to temperature variations, should receive three to five hours of full sun and some shade, especially in the afternoon. A tiny garden of Bok Choy can also be grown in containers.

Support, Depth, and Spacing

Seeds should be spaced 1/2 inch apart and 1/4 inch deep when planted. Plant seedlings 6 to 12 inches apart in the ground to provide enough growth. When you are planting rows of Bok Choy, keep a space of 18 to 30 inches between each row.

Cucumbers

There are different varieties of cucumber plants that you can grow. Some are grown on bushes and others on the vine. If you are planting a vine cucumber, then make sure to install a trellis in the raised bed to support the plant.

Sowing seeds is the most effective technique to plant any variety of cucumber. Before sowing the seeds, make sure the soil is warm enough. If the seeds do not germinate, they will freeze. Plant two-three seeds in the soil an inch deep. Sprouts will appear within a few days, usually one to two weeks following sowing.

Cucumber seeds should be spaced 20 to 36 inches apart when planted. Bushy cultivars, on the other hand, can be spaced closer together than vining varieties since their root systems do not run as deep into the soil.

Place the raised beds in a sunny location and amend the soil in the raised beds with compost. Before planting, check the pH of the soil; cucumbers prefer a neutral pH (6.5). Before planting, wait until the soil temperature reaches 70 degrees F. Light frosts will scorch or damage tender cucumber plants, so plan ahead. Supply the vines with a trellis or other form of support. Mulch the soil to let it retain moisture and keep it moist all of the time. The key to avoiding bitter cucumbers is regular watering. After the plants have begun to produce flowers, fertilize them. Cucumbers should be harvested frequently and carefully. If they grow too large, the plant will believe it has completed its task.

Peppers

There is another plant that can thrive in a raised garden bed: the pepper plant. You can experiment with different varieties of peppers. Following are some options that you can consider:

- Green bell pepper
- Red bell pepper
- Yellow bell pepper
- Cayenne pepper
- Jalapeno pepper
- Habanero Pepper
- Etc!

Peppers are not only a simple vegetable to cultivate, but they also add color to your garden. Sow the seeds in the pot to raise the seedlings. After the last spring frost, you can plant the pepper-plant seedlings outside in the garden. Raised beds, pots, and in-ground gardens are all good places to plant them. In a sunny, well-drained location, space them 18 to 24 inches apart. These plants require about 6-8 hours of direct sunlight each day to thrive.

Potatoes

The potato plant is another vegetable that flourishes in a raised bed garden. Raised beds provide you with complete control over the soil and nutrients, making potato care even easier. You can select a soil type that is best for your particular potato plant. It is simple to encourage healthy habits when you have this level of control.

Begin with disease-free, certified organic "seed" potatoes. Potatoes that have not been treated with a sprout retardant are known as seed potatoes. Only little potatoes, around the size of an egg, should be sown whole. Large potatoes should be cut into pieces with two or three eyes per piece. Sprouts grow from the tips called eyes. Allow the cuts or callous to dry for 24-48 hours before planting out to avoid rot. Loosen the soil to a depth of 8-10 inches with a garden fork. Incorporate a high-quality organic fertilizer into the soil as well. Dig a trench 6-8 inches deep for each row of seed potatoes.

Plant the potatoes at a distance of 12 inches on all sides. Now let nature do its work. You can harvest full-sized potatoes within 80-100 days of planting. Meanwhile, keep an eye on the plant and keep watering them properly.

Harvesting From Raised Beds

In some respects, the actual harvesting is easier in raised beds because you don't have to squat to remove the potatoes from the earth. The issue is that it's difficult to get a potato fork into the dirt without walking on it. To get your foot in place to step the potato fork deep into the dirt, you need to crawl up into the bed and stand on the side rail. The seed potatoes are about a foot deep, and the majority of the harvestable potatoes were 6-12 inches deep.

Zucchini

Vine-type zucchini cultivars are the best to plant. Planting zucchinis in a raised garden bed are beneficial not only to the plant but also to you! Your zucchini will be contained in a raised bed and will not spread and take over your yard. Most gardeners prefer to grow zucchinis in a bed on their own because these plants have spreading stems and wide leaves.

Directly sow zucchini seeds into the raised bed. These plants despise the cold and have a difficult time transplanting. Around five weeks after planting, your plant should start to vine. After sixty days or so, most zucchini cultivars are ready to harvest.

Types of Zucchinis to Grow

Zucchini comes in a variety of colors, sizes, and forms. However, all varieties provide the same nutritional value. Next are various zucchini variations.

1. Ambassador

Harvesting this cultivar takes 50 days. This sort of zucchini is dark green in color and cylindrical in shape.

2. Eight Ball

It takes 40 days to harvest this cultivar. This cultivar is dark green in color and has a globe-shaped form. It has a nutty, buttery flavor.

3. France White

This variety takes 50 days to mature after planting. This kind has a white tint and is excellent for a small garden.

4. Spacemiser

You may acquire the full tender size of this green hue veggie in 45 days. This tiny bushy plant will be able to provide you with many yields.

5. Seneca

This cultivar takes 42 days to mature. This type is dark green in color and cylindrical in shape.

6. Gold Rush

This type of zucchini matures in 45 days, which is comparable to other varieties. This type has a cylindrical form.

7. Costata Romanesco

This grey-green fruit has a nutty flavor with pale green flecks and has a fantastic taste.

How to Grow Zucchini

Zucchini is one of those easy-to-grow vegetables. You may enjoy the fresh taste or flavor of zucchini in your dish by following four simple steps.

Step One

Zucchini can be grown from seeds, but it is a delicate plant that cannot be transplanted. Wait until the latest frost date has passed before planting it. Once the last frost has passed, start sowing your seeds into the soil of your raised bed. Sowing seeds is simple; all of the directions are printed on the seed packet. Plant 2 to 3 seeds in each divot to increase the likelihood of germination. You can remove two or three plants from one hole after they have formed their first set of genuine leaves.

Step Two

You can't grow zucchini without pollinators. If you want to attract more pollinators to your vegetable garden, plant some attractive and colorful companion flowers, such as zinnias, cosmos, and calendula. Bees and butterflies will flock to these flowers in large numbers. If pollinators aren't attracted to your vegetable garden, you can utilize hand pollination as an alternative method of pollination. You'll need a small paintbrush for this, and all you have to do is delicately remove pollen from the male bloom and add it to the female blossom with your hands. This small effort will pay off in the shape of nutritious zucchini.

Step Three

The third step is to train the zucchini vines. It's vital to utilize a trellis if you're growing them on a raised bed. Zucchini has a tendency to crowd out other plants in your garden bed.

If you are growing them alone in a single raised bed, don't imagine you don't need a trellis since they won't disrupt the nearby plants. Use trellises anyway along the edge of the garden to the ground if you want to have good control over the zucchini plants.

This approach will be very useful since it expands the garden space and allows you to grow extra vegetables around the zucchini. Any plant requires water to survive. Because zucchini loves moisture, you should make it feasible to water them on a regular basis. The temperature of the soil and the amount of sunlight are two important factors to consider.

Step Four

Zucchini takes 45 days to mature after planting, and when they reach a length of about 5 to 6 inches, they are soft and easy to pick. If you wait until they are larger, they will turn woody and fibrous, which has a bad taste. Zucchini will be seedy, pulpy, and bitter in size. Because zucchini can grow 1 to 2 inches each day, you should be cautious while harvesting and check your plants every day. You can cut zucchini off at the stem with pruners or scissors or gently twist them off the stem; now, this healthful veggie is ready to eat.

Growing Tips

If you're new to gardening, there are a few pointers to keep in mind. They will help you get the most out of your gardening efforts.

Conditions of Growth

Before you plant zucchini, make sure you have all of the necessary conditions in place for it to produce well. To begin, select the finest location for your raised bed, ensuring that your plant receives full sun. The second requirement for zucchini is for the raised bed's soil to be rich and well-drained. You must consider the last expected frost date before beginning to grow zucchini. The third requirement is consistent irrigation, as zucchini prefers damp soil. They will not be able to produce nice fruit if the soil is dry.

Overplanting Should Be Avoided

Overplanting zucchini is a bad idea because each zucchini plant may yield 6 to 10 pounds of fruit over the course of the growing season.

The Pollination Process

Because zucchini plants have both male and female part flowers, pollination is a crucial aspect of their growth. In comparison to the female flower, which has an ovary and a short stem, the male flower has a long and slender stem. Pollination is carried out through bees and other insects. It's vital to note that this plant cannot bear fruit without pollination.

Feeding the Plant

Zucchini is a strong feeder that requires adequate nutrients from the soil. Compost and fertilizers should be used to fill the raised bed with organic matter. If your plant's leaves start to turn pale or appear feeble, it's time to treat it with compost and kelp fertilizers. You can also use a liquid fish foliar spray. Too much nitrogen is bad for zucchini plants since it reduces productivity, so avoid using nitrogen-rich fertilizers.

Watering

This plant needs one inch of water every week to keep the soil moist. Watering is especially important while the plant's bud is forming. Once your plants have established themselves, you may add a layer of mulch, such as straw or dried leaves, to help keep the soil moist and weeds at bay.

Plant your squash seeds only after the last frost has passed. It's best to wait a week after the last frost. Your squash seeds can be sown directly onto the raised bed. However, growing your squashes into a seedling first would be more beneficial. When the weather begins to warm up, you can then put the seedlings into your raised bed. It is suggested that to plant squash seedlings alongside a trellis. A squash plant growing on a trellis will benefit from improved air circulation. It's also easier to spot and monitor your squashes as they grow.

Alternatively, you can also plant a bushy squash plant. A bush cultivar is again a good choice for growing in a raised bed. They mature faster than other types of squash plants. Summer squash and winter squash are the two types of squash that are available.

Summer Squash Varieties

Squash grows swiftly in the summer. This variety takes roughly 60 days to mature. You may pick them all summer long, and the best part is that you can harvest them even when they are still young. Their skin is incredibly thin and delicate. Zucchini is the most common summer squash. Pattypan is the other summer squash type, and it is a delicious one.

Winter Squash Varieties

This type grows slowly; thus, patience is required when growing them. This variety takes 80 to 110 days to reach maturity. In comparison to summer versions, the winter squash's skin is thick and protective. They can be kept for a long time. Pumpkin, Hubbard, and butternut squashes are winter squashes. It's a big decision to pick the ideal variety for your raised bed. Here are a few well-known variations.

Acorn Squash

This particular cultivar has a delectable flavor. This variety's meat can be yellow or orange, and the skin is dark green with orange markings. This kind should be consumed within 2-3 months.

Buttercup

This type can be stored for up to 5 months. This cultivar has a texture similar to that of a potato. Because this is a vining type, train it to grow on a trellis.

Delicata

The skin of this cultivar is creamy yellow with green streaks. It's good for stuffing, steaming, and roasting. This will take up less room, but make sure you verify the variety because it comes in both bush and vining varieties.

Butternut

This kind is adaptable and may be used in soups, curries, and stir-fries. It requires little upkeep and prefers to spread out, so give it plenty of room.

Zucchini

Because this type has a bushy growth pattern, it requires a minimum of 4-5 feet to reach maturity. Zucchini can be used in stir-fries, curries, salads, and pasta dishes, as well as grated into cakes and bread.

Hubbard

It's a cultivar that can be preserved for up to six months. It's a bright addition because it comes in a variety of hues, including mild, blue, green, and deep orange. Similarly, it comes in a variety of sizes, ranging from a baby variety to a giant kind that weighs around 40 pounds and might pull your fence down if not supported.

Sugar Pumpkin

The best pumpkin is sugar pumpkin, which may be used in baking, soups, and pies. It's quite enormous, and you may keep it for three to four months.

Tomatoes

This juicy and delicious vegetable needs soil that is fertile and rich. Tomato plants are best to grow in raised beds. In a raised bed, you have more control over the amount and types of nutrients your tomato plant receives. Your growing tomato plant will need to be loosely tied to support. This is only required until the plant has grown all the way around it.

Vine Tomatoes in a Raised Bed

Support is required for vine tomatoes. Keeping this in mind when constructing the raised tomato garden will aid in determining where the raised bed will be placed and what materials will be used to construct the raised bed. A trellis or other support system can be constructed straight into the edges of the raised beds from the start, ensuring that even the most prolific, vigorous tomato vines are supported.

Grow Tumbling Tomato Varieties

Growing a tumbling tomato variety in the margins of your raised beds is a brilliant idea. Allow your raised beds' branches to flow over the sides.

Chives

Chives are a cool-season crop, which means they grow best in the spring and fall. The hotter temperatures of summer force them to hibernate until the weather cools down. In colder climates, sow chive seeds in a pot for 6 to 8 weeks before the last spring frost to gain a head start. Transplants the seedling in the garden then or plant seeds directly outside in the spring. Don't be surprised if they take a few weeks to germinate. For the best germination and growth, the soil temperature should be between 60-70 degrees F. Sow seeds no more than 1/4 inch deep and 2 inches apart. Apply a thin layer of dirt on top. Once the seedlings emerge, thin them out so that plants are 4 to 6 inches apart from all directions.

Garlic

When planting garlic, remember to cut the bulb apart and open it up. Each clove should be planted separately, with the pointed end facing up. The cloves require a time of cold in order to begin their growth process. You should plant your garlic in November. Allow enough time for your garlic cloves to mature before harvesting in the spring. Individual cloves should have grown into chubby new bulbs by now.

Improve Soil Conditions

Spread 1/2 to 1 pound of 5-10-10 fertilizer and 2 inches of compost over the top of the raised bed since the plant thrives in biologically rich soil. With a spade or hoe, work the fertilizer and compost into the top 6 inches of soil. After tilling, avoid stepping on the raised bed to prevent the soil from being compacted and losing its drainage ability.

Keep Proper Spacing

Individually cut the garlic bulbs into cloves. For planting, choose the large outer cloves from each bulb. With the pointy end facing up, push each clove 1 to 2 inches into the dirt and space them 3 inches apart in rows 10 inches apart. Because you don't have to walk between the rows to access the plants, garlic doesn't require broad row spacing in a raised bed.

Add Mulch

It is recommended to lay 4 inches of straw mulch over the top of raised beds while growing garlic. The mulch keeps weeds at bay while also retaining moisture. Mulch also insulates the soil in a raised bed.

Water Well

If there has been less than 1 inch of rain in the previous week, water the garlic once a week. In a raised bed, provide about 1 inch of water, or enough to saturate the top 6 inches of soil. If the temperature is above freezing and the weather is dry, continue to water throughout the winter.

Add Fertilizers

When the foliage reaches 8 inches tall in the spring, remove the mulch and sprinkle a 21-0-0 fertilizer beside each row of garlic, 6 inches from the base of the plants. Apply about a quarter cup of fertilizer per 20 square feet. After you've applied the mulch, make sure to water it right away and then replenish it.

Plant the Bulbs

Stop watering the plant when the foliage begins to turn yellow in early to mid-summer. Dig up the bulbs after half the leaves on each plant brown and begin to fall over.

As raised beds drain faster than standard beds, they may require more frequent watering in dry weather if the soil dries out faster. Harvest garlic and dry it for one to two weeks, or until the tops are totally dry and the skin around the bulbs is papery. Trim the tips and roots off the bulbs before storing them in a mesh bag in a cool, well-ventilated room.

Onions

Raised beds are also ideal for producing onions. These, among other veggies, are believed to be the easiest to grow. They need soil that is both well-draining and nourished. In raised beds, these two factors are simple to offer. Drainage is already provided by the raised bed. All you need to do is make a soil mix that is well-enriched! You can also use a premium-quality soil mix from the shop.

Fertilizer or even fresh compost can readily be added to your soil. Plant your onion seeds as soon as possible. It can take over a hundred days for these vegetables to reach maturity. Early in the spring is the optimum time to get started cultivating onions. This plant should be planted inside in a pot, and then you can transplant it once the final frost date has passed.

Green Beans

Green beans are a fast-growing crop that matures in around two months. This is true if you started your green bean plants from seed. Green beans aren't the only type of vegetable that may be produced in a raised garden bed; there are several varieties of beans that can be grown on raised beds:

- ✓ Blue Lake Bush beans
- ✓ Mascotte beans
- ✓ Dragon Tongue beans
- ✓ Yellow beans
- ✓ Purple beans
- ✓ Red beans

All bean plants deposit a significant amount of nitrogen into the soil in which they are produced. This makes them great vegetables to grow alongside other nitrogen-fixing plants. Cabbage and broccoli are heavy nitrogen-fixing plants. Green beans, like the other bean plants, thrive in warm conditions. They should be planted after the last frost has passed. You should space your bean seeds while sowing them in rows. Rows should be 18 inches apart. Each seedling in a row should be spaced about 2 inches apart.

Pumpkins

Pumpkins are grown on long vines that can reach a length of 20 feet or more. Pick a spot in a raised bed or garden where the vines will have lots of room to spread out. Plant pumpkins along the edge of a raised bed so that the vine maybe grow over it, and the rest of the bed can be used for other plants. When the vines are young, it's easy to direct them where you want them, but as they start to flower and set fruit, you'll want to leave them alone.

The number of days for the plant to mature is listed on the seed packet, which will assist you in choosing a variety that will grow and mature during your growing season. Make sure you have enough time between your average first and last frost dates if the variety you are planning to grow requires 110 days to mature. Pumpkins, like tomatoes and peppers, thrive in warm temperatures, so wait before planting outside until the weather has stabilized and there's no possibility of frost.

Planting and Harvesting Calendar for Vegetables

	Plants	When to Plant	When To Harvest
1	Kale	Spring or fall	60 days after planting
2	Tomatoes	After the last frost	60-85 days after planting
3	Chives	Early spring	60 days after sowing
4	Garlic	Late Sep-Nov	Lower Leaves turn brown
5	Onion	Early spring	Late summer-early fall
6	Beetroot	Early spring	7-8 weeks after planting
7	Pumpkin	May to early July	The fruit rind is firm
8	Squash	Spring	The fruit rind is firm
9	Zucchini	Early summer	55 days after planting
10	Potatoes	Early spring	60-90 days of planting
11	Cabbage	3-4 weeks before the last frost in spri	70-85 days after planting
12	Radishes	April, May, August	3 weeks after planting
13	Spinach	Late winter, early spring, later summer or early fall	37-45 days after planting
14	Cucumber	April-June	8-10 days after the first flower opens

Chapter 8: Top Fruits and Berries for Raised Bed Gardening

Imagine picking up juicy berries and grapes from your garden and serving them fresh! Doesn't that sound great? Well, now you can grow lots of different fruits in your raised bed garden, from strawberries to blueberries, apples, grapes, and melons, and enjoy their yields every season. Let me tell you when and how you can plant the most commonly used fruits and berries in your garden.

Strawberries

Strawberry plants thrive in raised garden beds. They give the necessary drainage for strawberry plants as well as the capacity to alter the soil quality in which your berries are grown. Raised garden beds also make it easier to maintain the plants. It's far easier to keep the berries safe from birds than it is to grow strawberries in the ground, and picking the berries doesn't take any bending.

A family of three can get enough berries from a regular 4-inch x 8 inch raised bed. Larger beds yield more berries, but a smaller 4-inch x 4 inch or 6-inch x 2-inch bed is ideal if you only want a handful of berries for your cereal every morning.

From early spring until early summer, you can plant new strawberry plants in your garden. If your new plants are in small pots, loosen the roots gently before planting them in the raised bed, especially if they were previously pot bound (roots circling around inside the pot). Spread the roots out a little into the planting hole, and make sure the crown is above the soil line and the roots are below.

Strawberry plants should be spaced 8 to 10 inches apart. Arrange the rows in such a way that each plant has plenty of area to grow. Provide consistent irrigation throughout the first year after planting, especially during periods of drought, to get the growing season off to a strong start.

Raspberries

Raspberries grow in climates with cool summers and moderate winters.

This plant is extremely susceptible to high temperatures; the ideal temperature for producing exquisite fruit is around 77 degrees F. It depends on where you live and what kind of climate you have.

You can start growing raspberries by purchasing one-year-old canes from a local nursery. Early in the spring, when the soil has warmed up, you can plant the raspberries. You can plant earlier and harvest sooner because you're growing in a raised bed. Raspberry plants can be planted in late autumn for a head start in milder climates. After the last frost, you may easily transplant the potted plants into your raised bed.

Raspberries can be purchased without pots or in containers for easy planting. The roots should be connected to the cane about an inch below the soil's surface. The raspberries in the raised bed should be planted to the same depth as the pot. Your plant will have to work harder to survive if you plant them deeper. A 3-foot spacing between two berry plants is required. The width of the raised bed must be at least 3 feet. Raspberry plants' roots need a lot of space to spread out.

Blackberries

Semi-trailing blackberries should be spaced 3 to 4 feet apart in raised beds while trailing blackberries should be spaced 6 to 8 feet apart. Blackberries thrive in full sun and well-draining, neutral to slightly acidic soil. They need extra water the first year after planting. The soil should always be moist 1 inch below the surface, with additional water supply during harvest. After the first year, weekly watering should suffice.

Blueberries

At least two distinct blueberry cultivar bushes that are suitable for your temperature zone should be purchased for sowing. Plant a lot of each variety to encourage cross-pollination. Dig holes that are 18 inches in diameter and 24 to several inches deeper than the length of the root systems of individual bushes. Fertilize each cultivar in accordance with the plant's needs and the cultivar's directions. Spread out the roots of each bush in its own hole. Soil should be added to the hole. Prepare the raised bed by filling it with topsoil that is 8 to 10 inches above ground level. Dig holes 18 inches in diameter and 24 to several inches deeper than the length of individual shrubs' root systems.

To avoid plant damage, leave a 3-inch-wide mulch-free zone around each individual plant. Keep the raised blueberry bed weed-free. Every 10 days, blueberries require 1 to 2 inches of water.

Gooseberries

Gooseberries may grow in a variety of soil types, although they prefer moist, well-drained soil. They do best in the sun and produce sweeter fruits, but will tolerate little shade as well. They can be grown in the ground or in huge soil-based compost containers. Plant bare-root gooseberries in late autumn or early spring and container-grown plants at any time of year, but avoid wet, dry, or cold soil. Bushes should be spaced 1.2–1.5 meters (4–5 feet) apart.

Raised beds provide you with more control over soil conditions and make it easier to harvest the grapes. A well-kept backyard grape arbor or tiny vineyard can be a lovely landscape feature. American grapes are more cold-hardy than most of their European relatives and may be grown in USDA plant hardiness zones 2 through 10.

For optimal results, plant grapes where they will receive full sun and sufficient air circulation. To avoid overpopulation, leave 6 to 10 feet between individual plants when planting, and pull all weeds as soon as they sprout. American varieties of grape plants thrive in soils with a pH of 5.5 or less and may not require further fertilizing if the soil is already enough for the plant's growth requirements. Soil testing can be done with the use of at-home testing kits.

Young grapevines should be watered once a week to encourage growth, but mature, deep-rooted vines can endure drought. Saturate the roots with water directly. Because of their large surfaces, grape leaves are prone to fungal infections. Make sure you don't get any water on them. To avoid overcrowding and ensure proper air circulation, space grape vines 6 to 10 feet apart.

Apply nitrogen fertilizer to the vines in the spring to promote quick development; this can be done with manure. Apply between 5 and 20 pounds of steer manure per vine to the soil in January or February. 5 to 10 pounds per vine is advised if poultry or chicken manure is employed. While this helps the vines to develop faster, be cautious that nitrogen fertilization can hinder grape growth.

Melons

Cantaloupe, watermelon, and honeydew melons are just a few of the melons that thrive in raised beds. They do require space to spread out. If given a chance, they will grow on vines that will stretch for several feet. The most difficult aspect of growing melons in a raised bed is making sure they get enough water. Melons contain a lot of water and, therefore, require a lot of it to grow effectively.

It's possible that the vines will spiral out of the garden beds and fall to the soil below. To reach peak flavor at harvest time, watermelon requires a lengthy, warm growing season and plenty of water. Starting the watermelon seeds indoors helps extend the growing season in locations with short summers, but utilizing black plastic mulch guarantees that your plants get the most out of the summer heat. Warming the soil with black plastic while avoiding weeds and conserving moisture is a win-win situation. The black plastic mulch also prevents the melons from setting directly on the soil, preventing pest and disease problems. In the spring, once all dangers of frost have passed, and the soil temperature has reached 65 degrees Fahrenheit, prepare the garden bed. Apply a 2-inch-high layer of compost to the bed and a starter fertilizer according to the package directions.

Apple Tree

Yes, you can plant fruits like apples in the raised bed garden as well. But planting trees in a soil bed is different from sowing seeds. In this case, you will have to grow the seeds into a baby tree in a container and then transfer them to the raised bed.

Wait until you're ready to plant before digging your hole. When you dig ahead of time, you run the risk of sidewall glazing, which occurs when the walls of a hole solidify.

This obstructs the proper development of the roots. Before planting, take a measurement of the root ball of your tree. You should only dig a hole that is an inch or two deeper than the root ball's length. When you plant your tree, you want the highest roots to be just below the surface.

The diameter of your hole should be at least twice the breadth of the root ball. Because the majority of the root system's growth will be lateral, excavating a large hole will make it easier to plant the root system effectively. The dimensions of depth and diameter are crucial. A hole that is too deep or too narrow may prevent appropriate root growth and cannot be fixed after the tree has been planted.

Carefully place your tree into the hole, spreading out its roots as you go. Remove your tree, widen the hole, and try again if there isn't enough room for the roots to grow out naturally without overlapping. As you fill the hole with soil, keep a firm grip on the tree to keep it upright. Tamp down the soil with your feet.

As you fill the hole, your tree will settle a little, but it should not sink. If it starts to sink, loosen the dirt, backfill the hole more solidly, and then press the soil more firmly as you plant. Water your tree slowly, but thoroughly, once it's in place. In your raised bed, a drip irrigation system or soaker hose will work effectively.

Planting and Harvesting Calendar for Fruits

	Plants	When to Plant	When To Harvest
1	Strawberries	Spring	4-6 weeks after
2	Blueberries	Early spring	June-August
3	Blackberries	Early spring	July-August
4	Raspberries	Early Spring	Early summer
5	Gooseberries	Spring	June to mid-July
6	Grapes	Later winter or early spring	When grapes turn green or yellow (white varieties) Or turns purple (red varieties)
7	Melon	10 days before last spring frost	Early June- August
8	Apple	Early Spring	Mid- Late August

Chapter 9:

Tips & Tricks for the Best Garden

The first planting season is going to be difficult. There are things that you can learn only by getting your hands dirty with the soil. But in a few months, you will feel like getting everything in control. There are certain measures that you can take to ensure the best results.

Select an Ideal Place

When it comes to starting a garden, it's all about location, just like it is with real estate. Place your garden in a visible spot in your yard so that you can see it regularly. You'll be a lot more likely to devote time to it if you can easily see it.

Follow the Sun

When you're first learning to garden, it's simple to make mistakes, like estimating the amount of sunshine. Before deciding where to put your garden, think about how the sun shines through your yard. To live, most edible plants, such as many vegetables, herbs, and fruits, require at least 6 hours of sunlight.

Keep Water in Proximity

One of the best gardening tips you'll ever get is to plan your new garden near a water source. Ensure that your garden may be connected to a hose so that you don't have to carry water to it every time your plants require it. The best way to see if plants need watering is to stick a finger one inch into the ground (approximately one knuckle deep). If the dirt is dry, it's time to water it.

Start with Quality Soil

When it comes to gardening, one of the most important pieces of advice is to invest in nutrient-rich, well-drained soil. If you're planning to plant in the ground, mix 3 inches of new Garden Soil into the top 6 to 8 inches of existing soil to get this specific blend. Use Raised Bed Soil if you're planting in a raised bed, as it has the appropriate weight and texture for raised bed gardening.

Go for Container Planting

Consider using containers if you're short on space. Many plants can be cultivated in pots, including vegetables, herbs, flowers, fruit trees, berries, and shrubs. When gardening in containers, use a pot large enough for the plant you're growing and fill it with soil mix. It not only helps potted plants thrive, but it also protects them from over-and under-watering.

Choose the Right Plants

It's vital to select plants that are appropriate for your growing environment. This means planting sun-loving plants in a sunny site, choosing heat-tolerant species in hot climates, and giving vines that eat the ground, such as pumpkins and melons, lots of space or a trellis to climb. Make your list and select varieties that will grow in the environment you live in and the space you have available. Start with young plants to get a head start, rather than trying to grow veggies and herbs from seed.

Discover Your Zone

Knowing your "hardiness zone" might help you choose the best plants for your needs. Simply put, it refers to the coldest temperature at which a plant can survive. The higher the zone number, the warmer the climate. As an example, if

a plant is labelled "hardy to zone 4" and you reside in zone 5, it will flourish in your garden. However, you won't be able to grow that particular plant if you live in zone 3 because it's too cold.

Determine where you fall in the hardiness zone. Here is the list of the zones and what you can grow in them:

- ✓ **Zones 1-2: Growing Season: April – September**

Vine tomatoes, lettuce, kale, broccoli, asparagus, eggplant, and other vegetables with a short time between planting and harvest are the best plants to grow.

- ✓ **Zones 3-4: Growing Season: April-October**

Vine tomatoes, lettuce, kale, broccoli, asparagus, spinach, strawberries, eggplant, sweet peas, pole beans, winter squash, and red and white potatoes are among the best plants to grow.

- ✓ **Zones 5-6: Growing Season: March-October**

Tomatoes, maize, squash, melons, beans, strawberries, lettuce, and other greens are the best plants to raise in the spring and fall.

- ✓ **Zones 7-8: Growing Season: March-November**

During the cooler months, the best plants to grow are corn, tomatoes, melons, squash, collard greens, carrots, bush beans, asparagus, and leafy greens.

- ✓ **Zones 9-10: Growing Season: February-November**

Tomatoes, squash, melons, peppers, corn, citrus, yams, figs, peaches, salad greens, bananas, and sweet peas are the best plants to grow during the cooler months.

- ✓ **Zones 11-13: Growing Season: Year-Round**

Kale, pineapple, pole beans, Okinawa spinach, passionfruit, sweet potato, red potato, cassava, pumpkin, mango, papaya, Thai chili peppers, citrus, bananas, and taro are some of the best plants to grow.

Learn your Frost Dates

It's risky to plant your garden too early (or too late) in the season. To avoid harming plants by putting them out too early, you'll need to know what the last usual spring frost date in your location is. Knowing when your first average fall frost date is can allow you to harvest or bring your plants indoors before the late-season cold kills them. Find out when your area's first and last frosts are forecast.

Frost days occur during the cold season between fall and spring when the weather is generally conducive to frost formation. This occurs in most of North America between October and March. Frost seasons are substantially shorter (or even non-existent) in some locations, whereas frost can occur at any time of year in others.

The average first frost date is the day in the fall when a frost is most likely to occur. The average last frost date for a location is the last day in spring when the area is typically frost-free at night. These are averages, not absolutes, for planning purposes. In any given year, there is a risk of frost occurring later than the average last frost date or sooner than the average first frost date.

Planting Zone	Last Frost Date	First Frost Date
1	May 22 – June 4	August 25-31
2	May 15-22	September 1-8
3	May 1-16	September 8-15
4	April 24 – May 12	September 21 – October 7
5	April 7-30	October 13 – October 21
6	April 1-21	October 17-31
7	March 22 – April 3	October 29 – November 15

8	March 13-28	November 7-28
9	February 6-28	November 25 – December 13
10-13	No freeze	No freeze

Add Mulch

Mulch each plant with a 2- to 3-inch-thick layer of mulch. You can reduce weed growth and moisture loss through evaporation by blocking off the light, needing less watering. For a polished look, lay down a layer of mulch. You may also use a straw, shredded leaves, pine straw, or any other readily available material.

What is Mulch?

Mulch includes all the materials that are used to cover the soil's surface and prevent its moisture from evaporating. Mulch is just fallen leaves and plant debris in nature. Compost, wood chips, rotting manure, cardboard, or even seaweed can be used as mulch in the garden.

Feed Plants Regularly

We've already covered the importance of starting with good soil, but that soil works best when it's regularly replenished with high-quality nutrients. To put it another way, a fantastic garden is made up of outstanding soil and high-quality plant fertilizers and compost.

Chapter 10:

Common Mistakes

You may have a vision or a dream about what you want to cultivate, but if you haven't evaluated whether or not that particular crop will thrive in your area, you're making a gardening mistake. Just because you like tomatoes. doesn't mean that you'll be able to grow them well in your location. Artichoke and okra are in the same boat. These are climate-specific plants that do not survive in all conditions. Planting crops that thrive in your area will help you achieve greater garden success. If you're not sure what grows well in your area, talk to a gardening neighbor and ask them what they've had success with.

Letting Weeds Get Out of Control

No one wants their weeds to grow out of control, but we don't always have a plan for removing weeds in place before we begin our garden. A classic gardening blunder is failing to take preventative measures against weeds in the garden. Keeping your weeds under control and getting rid of them before they grow out of hand or go to seed is essential for a healthy garden. Have a weeding method in place before you start planting your garden, so you'll be ready to go once the weeds appear.

Planting Too Large of a Garden

Another typical gardening blunder is planting a garden that is too large to handle properly. This is a common mistake made by first-time gardeners who are unaware of how time-consuming gardening can be. It's usually preferable to begin with a little garden and gradually increase how much you plant/grow. Year after year, expand your garden until it reaches a size that you and your family can handle.

Mono-Cropping

What is mono-cropping, and how does it work? It entails growing the same plant varieties over and over again with no variety or crop rotation. This is another typical gardening blunder that is often seen.

You must rotate where you put your crops in the garden each year if you want to cultivate the same crops year after year. Certain plants can deplete the soil's nutrients. Thus, it's critical to replenish the soil before replanting the crop. It would be even better to learn about companion planting, because what some plants take, others give back, and this strategy is really effective. Companion planting increases the biological diversity of the soil, resulting in healthier soil and making it more difficult for pests to detect the plants. You can also add flowers to your yard to help discourage pests.

Improper Watering

Another typical gardening blunder we encounter is individuals overwatering their gardens. Because they don't want the crops to dry up, many people tend to overwater. Plants, on the other hand, also require oxygen, and if your soil does not drain well enough, you may be smothering your plants without realizing it. Under-watering is another issue. You may think you're watering enough, but it's best to dig a little deeper to ensure that the soil is wet a few inches below the surface. It's also a good idea to dig down to make sure it's not too damp. It can be a tricky balance which is best learned through experience.

Too Many Chemicals

We all desire soil that is healthy and fertile. However, using too much herbicide, pesticide, fungicide, or even fertilizer can overload your soil with chemicals. Any amount of these compounds can be excessive. There are numerous alternatives to using chemicals to deal with pests and weeds. It's also vital to avoid using compost which is too hot, as this might add too much nitrogen to the soil and, in effect, burn your plants.

Planting Too Early or Too Late

We can get so enthusiastic about planting that we miss the right planting season for our area. Make sure you know when your region's first and last frost dates are so that you don't lose your crop due to poor timing.

Improper Spacing

Another typical gardening error is not understanding or ignoring the right spacing for the crops which you're cultivating. The seed packet suggestions are there for a reason. If you don't give your plant adequate room to grow, you can end up with a lower yield or perhaps a crop that dies because it is too crowded. The roots can become packed if they're planted too close together, limiting productivity. Planting too close together might suffocate the root system, resulting in the death of the plants.

Ignoring Soil Health

Thinking of your soil as nothing more than a structure to hold your plants is a common gardening blunder. Even with adequate watering, amending, and other practices, if your soil isn't healthy, neither will the plants grow. Building soil health is a long-term process. Throughout the year, as well as year after year, you must pay attention to your soil.

What you plant can help you build your soil in a variety of ways, as well as not making some of the common gardening mistakes listed above.

Wrong Location

Even experienced gardeners make the typical gardening mistake of placing their garden where it is most convenient for them rather than what is best for the crops they are planting. Consider the quantity of sunlight that your location receives when planning a garden and plant foods that will thrive in that amount of light. If your crops aren't doing well, attempt to figure out what's wrong. Are you shading too much or too little? Perhaps the plant is in a low spot where it collects and holds too much water, resulting in root rot.

Maybe it's because it's been planted too high and dry, and it's a crop that prefers a lot of water. Another problem with the location is that individuals tend to plant their gardens too far away from their homes. When your garden is out of sight, it might get neglected and "out of mind." You won't notice major issues if you can't check in on your garden on a regular (or many times daily) basis.

Planting Calendar

Yearly Summary

January	February	March
April	May	June
July	August	September
October	November	December

Planting and Seeding

Sr. No.	Plant Names / Identity	Planting Date

Planting and Seeding

Sr. No.	Plant Names / Identity	Planting Date

Companion Plants

Planting and Seeding

Sr. No.	Plant 01	Plant date	Plant 02	Planting Date

Planting and Seeding

Sr. No.	Plant 01	Plant date	Plant 02	Planting Date

Weekly Watering Planner

Plant Name	Mon	Tues	Wed	Thru	Friday	Sat	Sun

Plant Name	Mon	Tues	Wed	Thru	Friday	Sat	Sun

Plant Name	Mon	Tues	Wed	Thru	Friday	Sat	Sun

Plant Name	Mon	Tues	Wed	Thru	Friday	Sat	Sun

Plant Growth Progress

Plant Names	Jan	Feb	Mar	Apr	May	Jun	July	Aug	Sep	Oct	Nov	Dec

Garden Task and Planning

PRUNING												
Activities	Jan	Feb	Mar	Apr	May	Jun	July	Aug	Sep	Oct	Nov	Dec

SPRAYING

Plant Name	Jan	Feb	Mar	Apr	May	Jun	July	Aug	Sep	Oct	Nov	Dec

Harvesting Log

Sr. No	Plant Name	Expected Date

Harvesting Log

Sr. No	Plant Name	Expected Date

List of Gardening Tools

Tools	Checkbox
Garden Trowel	
Pointed Shovel	
Border Spade	
Nursery Spade	
Transplanting Spade	
Mini Pointed Shovel	
Mini Square Shovel	
Spear-Head Spade	
Root Assassin Shovel	
Root Slayer Shovel	
Metal Scoop Shovel	
Trenching Spade	
Drain Spade	
Claws Garden Gloves	
Spading Fork	
Bedding Fork	
Manure Fork	
Dibber/Dibbler	
Bulb Planter	
Wedger	
Auger Drill Bit	

Garden Spiral Hole Drill Planter	
Post Hole Digger	
Hollow Tine Aerator	
Power Core Aerator	
Digging Bar	
Hand Weeder	
Trowel Weeder	
Cobra head Weeder	
Wrotter	
Weeding Fork	
Grampa's Weeder	
Claw Weeder	
Weasel Weed Popper	
Cape Cod Weeder	
Japanese Weeding Sickle	
Long-Handled Weeder	
Dandelion Digger	
Korean Homi	
Oscillating Scuffle Cultivator Hoe	
Cultivator Hoe	
Crack Weeder	
Flame Weeder	
Steam Weeder	
Diamond Hoe	

Dutch Hoe	
Mattock	
Weed Trimmer	
Garden Scissors	
Garden Snips	
Pruning Shears/Secateurs	
Floral Shears	
Thorn Stripper	
Loppers	
Hedge Trimmer	
Hedge Shears	
Grass Shears	
Garden Knife/Hori Hori	
Box Cutter	
Reel Mower	
Electric Mower	
Edger	
Pruning Saw	
Harvest Sickle	
Billhook	
Hatchet	
Splitting Axe	
Bow Saw	
Pole Pruner	
Corn Broom	
Outdoor Push Broom	

Hand Whisk Broom	
Leaf Rake	
Groundskeeper Rake	
Bow Rake	
Landscaping Rake	
Thatch Rake	
Power Dethatcher	
Shrub Rake	
Hand Rake	
Leaf Blower/Vacuum/Mulcher	
Watering Can	
Garden Hose	
Spray Nozzle	
Water Breaker	
Watering Wand	
Hose Washers	
Hose Timer	
Drip Irrigation	
Sprinkler	
Gardening Gloves	
Kneeling Stool	
Kneeling Pad	
Knee Pads	
Tool Belt	
Wheelbarrow	
Garden Cart	

Carbide File	
Mallet	
Lumber Pencil	
Level	
Drill	
Multi-Tool	
Drum Roller	
Stripe Roller	

Conclusion

In a nutshell, one of the most productive ways to grow your own food is to use raised bed gardens. They allow you to have more control over soil conditions and harvest your crops more quickly and easily. Depending on your demands and the overall appearance you want to achieve, raised beds can be basic or fairly intricate. And through the text of this handbook, I tried my best to share many necessary facts, tricks and techniques to set raised bed gardens in a given space, from removing the grass to site preparation, building a raised bed to planting different fruits, herbs, flowers and vegetables together. There is a complete planting planner given at the end, which is perfect for writing your gardening-related activities in it. It is best to organize the plants in the raised bed according to different categories. It will help you keep track of all the plants and their growth cycle.

Made in United States
Troutdale, OR
09/27/2023

13239337R00084